Fundraising Analytics

Fundraising Analytics

Using Data to
Guide Strategy

JOSHUA
BIRKHOLZ

WILEY

John Wiley & Sons, Inc.

Library of Congress Cataloging-in-Publication Data:

Birkholz, Joshua.
  Fundraising analytics : using data to guide strategy / Joshua Birkholz.
    p. cm. — (The AFP fund development series)
  Includes index.
  ISBN 978-0-470-16557-7 (cloth)
  1. Fund raising. I. Title.
  HG177.B49 2008
  658.15'224—dc22

                                                                    2007049356

Printed in the United States of America
10 9 8 7 6 5 4 3 2

The AFP Fund Development Series

The AFP Fund Development Series is intended to provide fund development professionals and volunteers, including board members (and others interested in the nonprofit sector), with top-quality publications that help advance philanthropy as voluntary action for the public good. Our goal is to provide practical, timely guidance and information on fundraising, charitable giving, and related subjects. The Association of Fundraising Professionals (AFP) and Wiley each bring to this innovative collaboration unique and important resources that result in a whole greater than the sum of its parts. For information on other books in the series, please visit:

http://www.afpnet.org

THE ASSOCIATION OF FUNDRAISING PROFESSIONALS

The Association of Fundraising Professionals (AFP) represents 28,000 members in more than 185 chapters throughout the United States, Canada, Mexico, and China, working to advance philanthropy through advocacy, research, education, and certification programs.

The association fosters development and growth of fundraising professionals and promotes high ethical standards in the fundraising profession. For more information or to join the world's largest association of fundraising professionals, visit www.afpnet.org.

When any real progress is made, we unlearn and learn anew what we thought we knew before.

—HENRY DAVID THOREAU

How soon "not now" becomes "never".

—MARTIN LUTHER

Contents

Acknowledgments

The first acknowledgment I would like to make is to the people working in this most worthy field of fundraising. It is my privilege to learn from you every day. Your contribution to society is more than economic. It is the spark that ignites a generous spirit of change and opportunity. Be proud of this industry. You make a difference.

I wish to acknowledge the support and encouragement of my colleagues and friends at Bentz Whaley Flessner. I am especially indebted to the DonorCast team, Rachel Hurlbert, and Alexander Oftelie. Thanks are also in order to Judith Bourdeau, Katie Drossos, Tracy Gellman, and Sarah Billington for their substantial contribution. I could not do this without the trailblazing work of thought leaders such as Bobbie Strand and Terry Handler. A very special thanks to Bruce Flessner, a model of innovation, for his words.

Thanks are also due to Janet Hedrick for introducing me to Jan Alfieri and the great people at AFP. Thank you to the AFP publishing committee and to the team at John Wiley & Sons, Inc. I would like to pay a very special acknowledgment to Susan M. McDermott, Senior Editor. Thank you for all you did to make *Fundraising Analytics* possible.

As is only fitting, I would like to thank the donors to the campaign for building a beautiful, new Stillwater, Minnesota library. I hope my countless hours writing this book in the space you so generously funded enable many other organizations to connect with people like you.

I would like to thank God for leading me down this path. Thank you to my extraordinary daughters, Zoe, Charis, and Nora, for your unconditional love and support. And most of all, I would like to express my sincerest thanks to my wife, Tracy. Words cannot express how much I appreciate your love, sacrifices, and spiritual encouragement. I hope my actions forever reveal how much it means to me.

Foreword

It is easy to either overstate or underestimate changes in the fields of development and alumni relations. To many development professionals, the world of development has seen important changes, while to others the basics of the business have seemed to change little over their careers. One can make a strong case that the business of securing philanthropic support has long roots and that some of today's challenges are similar to those faced in years past. The letters of Paul to early Christian churches may be seen as early examples of fundraising letters, while the Cardinal of Milan's effort in the 14th century to get the merchants to organize themselves is an example of volunteer-driven fundraising. Tocqueville describing North America and Kropotkin observing Europe both noted the rise of voluntary associations as important social institutions.

Yet the world of development and constituent relations is not static. Change has come to the world of development. Some of the changes flow from economic shifts. We live in an era of growing dependence on very large gifts. Extraordinary levels of new wealth have given rise to a serious number of eight- and nine-figure gifts and have been a driving force behind the growth in the number of charitable foundations with their vast treasure of permanent charitable capital.

Other changes are social in nature. The rise in international giving reflects a new worldwide interest in sharing with all peoples and ensuring that the very poorest—those billions who still live on less than $1 a day—are able to receive the necessities they need. The increase of restricted giving reflects new generations'—baby boomers and Gen X—attitudes and skepticism toward institutions and toward their leaders' abilities to always make the right decision. These individuals want to control their philanthropic decisions.

Still other changes come from shifts in technology and knowledge. Automated phone banks, e-philanthropy, and bar-coded business reply envelopes are all examples of how technologies developed for other audiences and purposes have changed the world of development.

A generation ago, the emergence of computers revolutionized development offices. Large databases were now economically feasible to maintain and use, and activities such as simple segmentation by ZIP code, graduation class, or last year's gift were now easy to execute. Like the emergence of volunteer-driven fundraising and the creation of voluntary associations, data mining is the next great breakthrough in the fundraising industry. Its impact on development programs will be as great as any change in the past 50 years.

Josh Birkholz is one of the most sought-after speakers and writers in the field of development today. He is aptly positioned to lead us through this adventure of discovering the possibilities for applying the tools of analytics to advancement. Over the past decade, he has emerged as the leading practitioner and creative thinker in the world of analytics and philanthropy and has helped many of the nation's leading universities and medical centers build their own models and develop strong procedures. Additionally, he has launched DonorCast®, a new practice at Bentz Whaley Flessner that applies new analytical tools to a broad array of organizations.

The term "analytics" is tossed about frequently in many conversations inside development offices today, but the term has many different interpretations. For some, analytics is only about data mining; for others, it is about looking at statistical or mathematical applications inside advancement operations; and for still others, it is a tool drawn from predictive science. In this book, Birkholz walks us through the field of analytics, including all of its common uses, and in the end delivers a product that can be used by all development officers, not just statisticians. This is important because donor analytics is reshaping all areas of fundraising and constituent relations.

INSIGHTS FOR CAMPAIGNS

We live in the era of major campaigns. Billion-dollar campaigns no longer draw national attention, because so many institutions and causes seek extraordinary gifts to support their important work. As campaigns have grown larger, the importance of those handfuls of top gifts has also grown in importance. Today, the tools to identify gifts and donor behaviors are more important than ever. Birkholz helps to unlock important insights regarding these types of gifts.

BUILDING INVOLVEMENT

The best institutions know how to partner with their alumni, friends, and parents. Such success requires knowing constituencies and the variables regarding their interests and behaviors that are important. Once alumni and other institutional supporters are understood, it is possible to track their involvement—which includes giving, advocacy, linkages, and volunteering. Birkholz helps us use tools to improve the effectiveness of alumni relations and constituent relations programs.

BROADENING OUR SUPPORT BASE

Analytics in all its forms, including data mining, donor modeling, and pattern analysis, is already reshaping the world of fundraising and alumni relations. It is the greatest breakthrough in annual giving since automated phone banks arrived in the late 1980s. For the past several decades, while many new techniques have been introduced or refined, national results of annual giving programs have been disappointing.

The lifetime of relationships that reflects itself in yearly gifts to the annual fund has many dimensions, but analytics will be a critical tool in the program. Analytics can help identify key characteristics signifying when people are ready to start giving. It can also help development offices understand the patterns of behavior and involvement that are critical to donor retention and upgrading.

The new tools of analytics, when combined with centuries of insights about private gift support and volunteering, open new possibilities to build upon the current practices of fundraising and to further the important work of philanthropy.

Analytics will not make fundraising wholly new; the pioneering work of Si Seymour will continue to guide us. Yet, one can imagine how much more Seymour's fundraising ventures might have achieved if the tools of technology and the insights of analytics had been available during the 1940s and 1950s. Seymour would not have stood for a world that was "wholly old" when such breakthroughs were possible.

Birkholz understands the traditions of philanthropy and its great impact on donors and recipients; he also understands the tools of analytics. The combination is powerful. The promise of analytics is not that it is a wholly new concept, but rather that its tools let us meet the agenda of past generations effectively.

When I was a young development officer at Kalamazoo College, I remember the week that a sophomore student was tragically killed in an accident. The campus community gathered at Stetson Chapel for the service to remember the life of the young man. Dr. George Rainsford, the College's President, rose slowly from his seat and walked to the front of the packed sanctuary. He began his address with the powerful words, "An alma mater knows her children one by one."

For three decades I pondered those words. How could colleges and universities know their children—not as a mass group or a few subsets of a mass group—but as individuals? In turn, I began to think about how we could best engage our alumni and involve them in the life of the institution—as donors, volunteers, advocates, and partners.

Analytics may not take us all the way to knowing each alumnus as an individual, but it is the most powerful tool in our lifetime for helping every institution, every alma mater, to know her children one by one.

This is the most important book for anyone who cares about securing private gift support.

Bruce W. Flessner
Founding Principal
Bentz Whaley Flessner

Overview of Fundraising Analytics

There is a fundamental change emerging in 21st-century fundraising. This change is not driven by increasingly sophisticated nonprofit organizations; nor is it propelled primarily by the integration of MBAs or other smart people into the sector. Not even the compelling need for support of worthy causes produced this evolutionary leap. In fact, it is the most important component of the philanthropic partnership that is moving us forward: We are changing because of our donors.

Donors approach philanthropy in a completely different way. They make decisions more thoughtfully. Their gifts follow their own intended purposes. Donors seek a return on their philanthropic investments. And they desire an increased level of personalization.

Organizations embracing this change are climbing a mountain of success without zenith, while others, forcing their own models onto their donors, are fighting in the foothills. In this time of great wealth and generosity, I wish the mountain of success for you. But more importantly, I wish to see the worthy causes you represent feed our world, educate our children, wipe out horrible diseases, and accomplish many good things. That is why I wrote this book.

As a fundraising strategist and student of philanthropy, I see tools and techniques consistently produce wonderful results. I have seen these same tools and techniques fail. When we put our hope in devices and skills without an appropriate focus on donors, we rarely succeed. As I present an approach to using *data* to guide strategy, I hope you realize that I really intend for you to use *people* to guide strategy. But these are not just any people. These are the people who care passionately for what you do. Likely, you share this passion, or you would not be where you are.

Every person has a thing, a person, or an idea they cherish. For most people, there are many things, people, and ideas. Things might include home, community, or an heirloom. People might include significant other, children, all children, or the poor. Ideas might include peace, education, religion, artistic expression, and health. This treasured grouping of things, people, and ideas might be called a person's *value portfolio*.

Everything a person does in life in guided by his or her value portfolio. It is the reason people work. It is the object of their leisure. It is what they pass on to their children. And, most importantly for this book, it is the beneficiary of their philanthropy. Donors do not give to you; they give to their value portfolios.

Every nonprofit organization also has a value portfolio. This is the purpose of what they do. This is the reason they exist. This is where they spend the gifts they are given. When the value portfolios of a donor and an organization align, an interchange of investment and impact is the result. This is the key to successful, major gift fundraising.

Obviously, using this key requires something of us. First of all, we need to understand the value portfolios of our donors. Next, we need to understand the value portfolio of our organization. Then, we need to bring them together.

Analytics is a suite of metrical tools and techniques for understanding the past and projecting the future. For analytics to be effective, we must use it in the context of our work. Most importantly, it must be used in the context of our donors.

We can use analytics to understand the value portfolios of our donors. Why do they give to us? Who is most aligned to our value portfolio and warranting attention? Which field officers most effectively position which portions of the value portfolio? Which prospects have other or even contrasting values? Are we spending the right time with the right prospects using the right field officers?

We can use analytics to understand our fundraising programs. How do we spend our time? Which of these tasks contribute to increased giving? Which tasks detract from fundraising success? Are we subject to the right metrics? Are we using metrics at all?

We can use analytics to pave our road for the future. Which prospects will be our top donors 10 years from now? How many new field officers should we hire? Will our infrastructure support this growth? What should our campaign goal be? Is it attainable? What are the factors for our success?

Using data to guide strategy is more than just database technology. It is the core of what we do. Essentially, we are using people to guide strategy. We are using our values to guide strategy. We are using the values of our people to guide strategy. And, most importantly, our strategy is grounded in facts, not assumptions.

DEFINING ANALYTICS

In the fundraising industry, many diverse definitions of *analytics* can be found. Largely, this is because many vendors doing business in the non-profit market describe their product offerings as analytics. Often, each vendor offers a portion of the broader services generally associated with the term. Some vendors provide predictive modeling in combination with database screening services. Others may conduct market research studies to determine attitudes and giving motivations. And still others provide metrical assessments of annual giving or membership programs. All of these services are analytics, but rarely do you see all of these services in one place.

I would describe analytics as a suite of statistical tools and techniques used to:

- Analyze constituencies
- Build models to predict constituent behaviors
- Make organizational decisions by:
  - Evaluating program performance
  - Projecting future program performance

It is likely you have heard many accounts of corporations analyzing their customer base. Corporations such as Best Buy, J.P. Morgan, and Volkswagen have conducted thorough analyses of who purchases their products and services and why they make these purchases. These descriptive analytics studies generally focus on demographics, geography, behaviors, transactional history, and interests. The goals of these projects are to produce a taxonomy of key groups. Then they market and engineer their products and services with these taxonomies in mind.

When a higher education development office develops custom strategies for alumni, young alumni, community members, and faculty, they are using similar customization. When a health care organization approaches patients differently than community donors, they also use similar customization. However, these are natural organizational segments. There may be many other derived segments informed by demographic characteristics, entry points, giving motivations, occupation, industry, and affinities. These characteristics may warrant revised segmentation strategies.

Many of us most often interact with a predictive model when we seek financial services. The credit score or FICO score, named for the Fair Isaac Corporation, is an everyday example of a predictive model. These scores predict a statistical likelihood of loan repayment. As a result of analysis of the characteristics of those who do and do not pay back loans, the credit score statistically predicts how likely you are to pay back your loan. When a lender chooses to give you a loan, they made the decision based on your financial ability and likelihood to pay.

In fundraising, major gift officers assess their portfolios according to financial ability, or *capacity,* and the likelihood of making a major gift. This likelihood is informed by the prospect's connection to the organization and/or an alignment of interests between the organization and prospect (matching value portfolios). This assessment is made through interpersonal interaction. Prospect researchers will also seek out capacity and likelihood information in their data gathering and interpretation. Also, at the individual level, prospect research informs the capacity to give and the likelihood of making a major gift. However, unlike the financial services industry, most organizations filter their base using transactional history (previous giving) and/or capacity information alone. The concept of likelihood is rarely used to prequalify potential donors in advance of prospect research or even roll-out to the frontline gift officers.

Not long ago, large banking corporations needed ways to assess the performance of many branches using simple yet very relevant reports. The result of this need was the emergence of scorecards. These one-page reports highlighted the key areas of performance as they related either directly or indirectly to branch success. An executive could quickly compare branches using these documents.

If you are a baseball fan, you can quickly determine how teams and specific players are performing by reviewing statistics in the newspaper.

These similar analytics strategies may also be used to gauge the effectiveness of your fundraising program. If you monitor your acquisition, renewal, and reactivation rates, you are using statistics as a performance monitor. Are you also considering the yield rates of your gift officers, the ratio of ask amounts to capacity ratings, the production efficiency of your prospect researchers, or the diversification of your prospect portfolios? Some sophisticated fundraising organizations are developing scorecards of their own to monitor gift officer and program performance. These scorecards, more commonly known as *dashboards* in this industry, can be very effective if the metrics truly indicate performance.

When very large and complex corporations make budgetary decisions, they need to account for knowns and unknowns. For example, they must consider employee turnover rates, changes in market demand, variation in the stock market, shifting energy prices, competitor penetration, and so on. To prepare for the possibilities, they will incorporate simulation models. These techniques will project what is expected and what might happen, accounting for numerous parameters. Based on these models, they will determine the most likely results based on the scenarios and impact of potential shifts in the parameters.

In determining comprehensive campaign totals, you should consider your knowns and your unknowns. You should consider current production, yields in relation to capacity, the impact of staff turnover, steady income streams (annual giving and membership), variable income streams (major giving), the stock market, giving likelihoods of key constituents, aggregate affinities of the base, and so on.

A substantial difference between the for-profit and the nonprofit use of analytics is who conducts the analysis. Is it in-house or outsourced? Up until about 25 years ago, most campaign management was outsourced to residential consultants. They would come in, manage the campaign, and leave upon its conclusion. Rarely would the campaign management skills develop in-house. Nowadays, consultants, similar to for-profit business consultants, will still typically conduct studies and program audits but will also build internal capacity to manage the campaigns. In analytics, the business world is building this capacity in-house. However, most nonprofits continue to outsource this work. This shift to building internal analytics and data mining programs in-house is very much in its infancy for the nonprofit world.

THE MIND OF AN ANALYST

To set the stage for a conversation about analytics, I want to let you into my world. I might think of myself first as a fundraising consultant. Certainly, this is true. I am a consultant with the well-respected national fundraising consulting firm, Bentz Whaley Flessner (BWF). BWF has been behind some of the largest and most influential fundraising campaigns of our era. The thought leadership of this firm has contributed volumes of strategic literature and methodologies for major gift fundraising, prospecting, and relationship management.

I might also call myself a data miner. Certainly, this is true, too. I built predictive models as an analytics professional for the University of Minnesota. I continue to engineer data mining programs throughout the United States. And, I am invited to speak about integrating data mining into the fundraising process throughout the year.

However, I consider myself a student of fundraising. Specifically, I study the economics of fundraising. I have great curiosity in the matters of consequence for the development industry. How do things work? Why do we do what we do? How can we do it better? How can this world be better?

I might be a bit curious about inconsequential things as well. My mother reminds me that as a young child I was very curious. When I was in my primary years of school, I enjoyed overhauling household appliances. In the first grade, I was able to fix our troublesome vacuum cleaner on several occasions. In the fourth grade, I made a radio out of the parts of an old electric organ in my grandfather's garage. In high school, I would create musical instruments out of our household items. I wanted to know how these things worked.

This did not stop as an adult. When I discovered they were making a movie out of a favorite childhood book, *The Lord of the Rings,* I was quite enthused. I requested a vacation day from work for the release date. And, I began to think about the factors for enjoying a film. In fact, I decided to learn about the metrics and build a model to optimize my experience.

I began my *"Lord of the Rings* model" by thinking about the moviegoing experience. Often, when I know a lot about the backstory or the history of a movie, I enjoy it more than when I know nothing about it. The atmosphere produced by the people in the room can contribute to the experience. The movie itself needs to have a strong story, convincing production quality, effective acting, and well-composed music. The setting must provide superior delivery of the audio and visual elements. And the logistics of purchasing tickets, driving to the theater, and waiting in line also can contribute positively or negatively to the experience.

After understanding the movie experience, I needed to determine the data elements related to these various factors. Some of the data elements could not be measured. I needed to make decisions about them based on my personal experience. Other elements were measurable and could be researched. The following table compares the factors to the data elements.

Moviegoing Experience Factors	Related Data Elements
The backstory or history	• Quality of initial book • Fan blogs and discussion forums
The people in the room	• Favorite theaters of hard-core movie fans (measurable) • Times different types of moviegoers attend (measurable)
Strong story	• Writers • Source material
Production quality	• Film budget (measurable) • Reports from production magazines • Crew members
Effective acting	• Actors involved • Director
Well-composed music	• Composer
Setting: Audio	• Theater sound system (measurable) • Number of speakers (measurable) • Size of speakers (measurable) • Purchase date of speakers (measurable)
Setting: Visual	• Digital versus film projection (measurable) • Lumen readings on the screen (measurable) • Frequency of changing the projector bulbs (measurable) • Recency of changing the projector bulbs (measurable)

(Continued)

Logistics	• Online versus in-person ticket purchasing (measurable)
	• Estimated wait times for other blockbuster premieres (measurable)
	• Proximity from home (measurable)

At this point, I felt I had a solid understanding of the moviegoing experience and the related data elements, but I had not yet set the stage for my model. To do this, I had to determine specifically what I wanted to accomplish and how I would prepare the data to do this. Since I had already decided to select this particular movie, my question was about optimizing the experience for a movie I had already selected. This reduced my data elements to items that were neutral as to the selection.

After understanding the movie experience and the data involved, I needed to gather and prepare the data for modeling. I created a spreadsheet and began filling the cells with information. The technology specialists from the various theater chains had never received phone calls of this type. In fact, one specialist told me he would change the bulbs in the Minneapolis-area theaters the week of the release date because I asked!

I combined the data and evaluated my model. I went to the field and tested some theaters on other movies. Some theaters had strong sound systems but small, dark screens. Others had older sound systems with crackling speakers but beautiful visual presentations. A few wonderful theaters were too far for driving home from a midnight showing. This testing helped me narrow in on my ultimate choice. I chose a theater with new bulbs, optimal lumen readings, a new sound system, 12-mile proximity from my house, and an estimated wait time of two and one-half hours (the average for theaters of this caliber was closer to six hours).

Finally, I deployed my model. First, I communicated the results to the various online message boards and blogs to share my success with other Minneapolis-area *Lord of the Rings* fans. Then, I purchased my tickets and waited for about three and one-half hours to see the 12:01 showing. When I watched the movie, I had a wonderful time and left the theater smiling.

Perhaps this level of attention to a movie is overkill and ultimately unnecessary. However, this was a valuable exercise in learning the steps of the Cross Industry Standard Process for Data Mining, or CRISP-DM

(Exhibit 1.1). This process, which I reference several times throughout the book, has six primary steps.

Step 1. *Business Understanding:* Defining the context of the analysis
Step 2. *Data Understanding:* Aligning data elements to the context
Step 3. *Data Preparation:* Gathering and priming the data for analysis
Step 4. *Modeling:* Conducting the analysis
Step 5. *Evaluation:* Determining whether the analysis supports the goal of the business understanding
Step 6. *Deployment:* Implementing the analysis

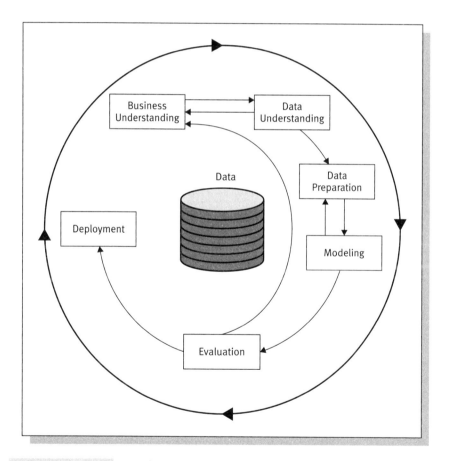

EXHIBIT 1.1   **CROSS INDUSTRY STANDARD PROCESS FOR DATA MINING (CRISP-DM)**

Here is a comparison of the CRISP-DM steps to the *Lord of the Rings* model.

CRISP-DM	Lord of the Rings Model
Business Understanding	Understanding the moviegoing experience
Data Understanding	Understanding the data elements that contribute to this experience
Data Preparation	Refining the data pool and gathering elements
Modeling	Computing the scores
Evaluation	Testing the model by attending various theaters
Deployment	Showtime

This methodology of predictive modeling will become so natural to an analytics professional that projects like the *Lord of the Rings* model will be common. This is the mind of the analyst. Much like how artists use form and function to communicate an idea, analysts use form and function to understand a concept. The best of us are both insanely curious and remarkably methodical. These qualities led J.S. Bach to equal temperament. They instilled the composer, Charles Ives, with an exceptional business mind. They moved Seurat to foreshadow the concept of the pixel. Even video game makers like Valve sought to understand the physics of gravity to make a more realistic game out of *Half Life 2*. These are the same qualities that lead people like Steven Levitt to analyze sumo wrestling, Daniel Pink to study the new conceptual age, and for me to model the *Lord of the Rings*.

Now, take this seemingly inconsequential curiosity and move it into the realm of the consequential. Arguably, among such pursuits, charity is perhaps of the greatest consequence. Human generosity has healed diseases, fed millions of people, and contributed to a better life for all of us. Why do people give? Why do they give to us? Who will never give to us? Why are some charities more successful than others? What can we do differently?

Analytics is not a science of numbers; it is a science of "why." This is the method of soothing insane curiosity about our business processes and our constituencies. This is how we can look at what we do and change what we will do. Analytics uses our data to guide us down a path of optimized performance and increased productivity.

My goal in this book is to advance a deep respect for your donors by incorporating the techniques of analytics and the perspective of a fundraising economist. To accomplish this, I have structured the text in a way that enables specific applications to various programs and strategies within most fundraising departments.

WHAT TO EXPECT

Over the next eight chapters, I hope to address all the primary audiences of a book on fundraising analytics. Some of you are fundraising executives and managers. You will have questions about how analytics will make your organizations better: Will it increase production? Will it help us be more efficient and thus better stewards of the budgets entrusted to us for fundraising? Some of you are field fundraisers interested in better connecting and engaging with your portfolios of prospects. Some of you are prospect researchers. Analytics has become part of the skill set in your world. You may have concerns about staying competitive in the job market or managing new analytics professionals reporting to you. Some of you might be annual giving professionals trying one more technique to boost your participation rate. And some of you might be career statisticians learning about the fundraising industry. I hope I can say to all of you, "This book is for you."

I have designed it to cover the primary applications of analytics in Chapters 2 through 6. This is a combination of big-picture context, application, cases, and implementation suggestions. Chapters 7 through 9 are designed to be "how-to" chapters for the practitioners. An executive can read through Chapter 6 and be confident in the concepts. Staff analysts or professionals looking to learn analytics skills will benefit from the step-by-step instructions in the final chapters. Here is a summary of what you will read.

Chapter 2: Understanding your Constituents

A primary component of analytics in fundraising is understanding who gives to you, why they give to you, and what you are doing about it. The corporate world has a detailed understanding of the primary customer groups that purchase their products. Most executives can rattle off their primary markets and their levels of penetration. Most fundraising executives know several members from the top of their pyramid and their board, but they struggle to categorize their base for support. They know the people who make their presence known at the personal level, but do they know the full story? Why would a person give to your organization? Do you really know?

This chapter explores the concepts of descriptive analytics to understand your constituency. It discusses everything from demographics to giving motivations to help you ask the right questions. And those right questions concern your donors.

Chapter 3: Analytics and Prospecting

Analytics has seen the most growth in recent years among the prospect development function of sophisticated fundraising organizations. It is a very effective means of identifying potential prospects for major and planned giving. Many directors of prospect research are urged to build this capacity in their organizations. Sometimes, this push is driven by board members seeing the success of incorporating analytics into their companies. For many prospect researchers, this may seem threatening; it does not need to be.

In this chapter, I discuss the concepts of prospecting and fit analytics into that context. If you are completely unfamiliar with prospecting as a discipline, this chapter should be informative to you. If you are a seasoned prospecting professional, you will understand why analytics is growing up all around you.

Chapter 4: Analytics and Campaign Planning

The comprehensive campaign has taken on a life of its own in the fundraising world. For many of us, planning and executing a campaign will be among the biggest stretches in our careers. As your need to execute challenging campaign strategies increases, your need for strategic allies increases. There is no better ally than your data. When it is on your side, you know you are doing the right things.

This chapter explores campaign planning from the context of constituency potential, effectiveness of strategies, and your ability to execute these strategies. Basic techniques for campaign planning, including capacity analysis and pyramid design, are also shown.

Chapter 5: Data-Driven Prospect Management

One of the most telling indicators that an organization is data driven is having a systematized method of connecting with and engaging constituents. Organizations that do this well raise a lot of money. Those that don't might get by on luck—but I don't see it too often. Data-driven prospect management will transform your institution if you do not already have it in place.

In this chapter I devote considerable attention to covering prospect management from the basics to the development of metrics. I also include a detailed work plan for building a data-driven prospect management system for your organization. It is critical for an analytics professional to understand prospect management thoroughly. It is the business context of fundraising.

Chapter 6: Annual Giving Analytics

For an analytics professional, annual giving and membership programs provide the greatest opportunities for seeing the data in action. Models predicting responses to appeals can be tested and evaluated in a matter of weeks. By shifting the attention on the constituents most likely to respond to your messages and minimizing the attention to those who will never respond, you can be more efficient in your base development activities.

Chapter 6 will discuss principles of segmentation, modeling, and developing metrics to gauge and guide your success. Whether you are outsourcing your analytics or building in-house capacities, you will be equipped to make better decisions guided by your data.

Chapter 7: Selecting Data for Mining

The first step for any analysis project is producing your data file. Modern prospect relationship management databases have countless fields to explore and incorporate into models.

This chapter presents a field-by-field guide to the fields you might extract for analytics. If you are new to analytics, this will be a helpful guide to navigating the possibilities in your database.

Chapter 8: Descriptive Analysis: Basic Statistics and Scoring Models

Whether statistics is new or "old hat" to you, it is helpful to see some of the basic statistical operations in action on a fundraising database. After discussing the many applications of analytics in the preceding chapters, you might be wondering, "Where do I start?"

In this very specific how-to chapter, many of the basic statistical techniques using Statistical Package for the Social Sciences software (SPSS) are demonstrated. Expect to see how to conduct descriptive analysis, build simple scoring models to rank correlation, build an RFM score (recency, frequency, monetary values), and build a basic attachment score.

Chapter 9: Regression Analysis

Very powerful statistical tools for predictive analysis are now within your reach. Statistical software has become very user friendly. Complex regression analysis used to be left to the academic statisticians. Now you too can produce predictive models to identify major and planned gift donors, segment a mail file, or prioritize your constituency.

This chapter presents step-by-step instructions for building a model to predict giving at your organization. I use SPSS to demonstrate a binary logistic regression formula and evaluate the results. After learning this technique, building models of many varieties will be within your grasp.

Glossary of Common Terminology

At the end of the book, I've assembled a brief glossary of some of the common terminology used in fundraising analytics. Throughout the book, I have tried to remain free from jargon, but sometimes there are no other words for the peculiar things we do. For this reason, I have tried to decode the code for many of you who might be new to this field.

ENJOY THE JOURNEY

I hope you enjoy your journey into the exciting world of fundraising analytics. Don't feel overwhelmed by the many different concepts presented in this book. You should not worry about applying all of these techniques overnight. As you read, keep a journal of new ideas. When you are finished, go back to the journal and organize it into strategies you can apply now, strategies for the three-year plan, and strategies warranting long-term discussion. Then try one thing at a time. Get a license for statistics software. Run some basic correlations. Focus on enhancing your database with new data. Evaluate your business processes.

As long as your focus remains on the donor, your data-driven strategies will evolve to benefit your organization. To be guided by data means to be guided by donors. Donors are the remarkable coefficients in high-results equations. If you plug them into your formula, your results will be extraordinary.

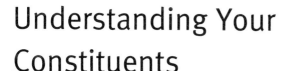

CHAPTER 2

Understanding Your Constituents

Perhaps the most important questions a fundraiser should ask are:

- Who are our donors?
- Why do they give to us?

Of all the questions I might pose as a consultant, these are the two that most often produce assumptions. Rarely do I find an organization that truly understands the uniqueness and the diversity of its own constituents. How would you answer these questions?

In the first chapter, I introduced the idea of natural segments vs. derived segments. I developed this distinction to separate those segments of your constituency you have always considered from those you might consider. Here are a few examples of natural segments.

NATURAL SEGMENTS

Natural Segments Common to Most Nonprofits

Most fundraising programs observe giving-related segmentation. In base development programs such as membership or annual giving, the natural segments are non-donors, new donors, LYBUNTs (gave last year but unfortunately not this year), lapsed or SYBUNTs (gave some year but unfortunately not this year), long lapsed, and major donors (generally defined by a dollar amount). Higher education, health care, and the arts will frequently observe additional natural segments.

Natural Segments in Higher Education

The most obvious segment in higher education is the alumni population. Higher education enjoys this direct feed of constituents into their database. Many base-development strategies are geared around engaging and teaching philanthropic behavior to alumni. However, at many universities and some colleges, the non-alumni population or "friends" of the institution will often match or exceed the philanthropic dollars of the alumni at the major gift level. Other natural constituencies may include corporations, foundations, faculty, and staff.

Natural Segments in Health Care

Health care organizations that provide patient care also enjoy a direct feed of constituents. Although HIPAA provides restrictions about knowing diagnoses, these fundraising organizations can reach out to their patients. These organizations also benefit from the support of community members, hospital staff, and volunteers.

Natural Segments in the Arts

Attendance at performances and visits to museums are generally captured at most arts organizations. In the performing arts, membership usually refers to season-ticket holders—another natural segment. In public broadcasting and museums, membership may refer more to giving participation. Arts organizations benefit from natural associations with programming knowledge. For example, a symphony will know if a person generally attends Baroque, pops, or contemporary concerts. A public television station will know if a member pledged during a Lawrence Welk or Suze Orman program.

PORTFOLIO ASSIGNMENT

Other natural segments will influence the assignment of prospects into major gift officer portfolios. In my experience, I have found three predominant methods of making these assignments:

1. Program-based assignments
2. Region-based assignments
3. Political-based assignments

In program-based assignments, a major gift officer will have a portfolio of prospects for specific disciplines or fields of research. For example, a gift officer may have all prospects for an engineering program at a school. Another gift officer may have English prospects. In a research organization, a gift officer may have an entire portfolio of prospects for cancer research, while another may have metabolic diseases.

Organizations that assign prospects to portfolios based on regions generally maintain a national presence. They might give one gift officer all of the prospects for the Pacific Northwest, while another gift officer manages New England. In a local nonprofit, you might also see gift officers assigned to specific communities. For example, one gift officer might work St. Paul, while another works Minneapolis. One gift officer might work the outer boroughs, while another works Manhattan.

Almost all nonprofits have some political reasons behind their assignments as well. The most common has to do with giving level. A multi-millionaire prospect might only work with the very top executive of the nonprofit. Also, the risk of not closing a high-level gift might be too high for assigning a prospect to a junior-level gift officer.

All three of these predominant methods stem from efficiency and risk management. In program-based assignments, it is more efficient for one person to learn everything there is to know about a program. This way, they are best able to communicate with the program's natural constituents. In region-based assignments, there is an efficiency of travel costs. In political-based assignments, the efficiency has more to do with yield rates.

For an organization to try alternative approaches to assignment methods, it must demonstrate an increase in efficiency and/or production. Analyzing the best segmentation for assignments and tuning the distribution of prospects assigned to a gift officer is known as *portfolio optimization*. To optimize a portfolio, you need to be equipped to expand your segmentation ability. Similarly, expanding and refining your segments will strengthen your ability to optimize broadbased solicitation activities.

DERIVED SEGMENTS

Analytics can help you to broaden and refine your understanding of your donors and their motivations. Using techniques such as constituent research and descriptive statistics, you have limitless possibilities. Although the specific characteristics and motivations of your donors will be unique to you, two groupings of segments across all industries are prevalent:

Group 1: Income versus Assets
Group 2: Philanthropic Motivations

Income versus Assets

Across nonprofits of every type, one can find donors making philanthropic decisions based on either their cash flow situation or their assets. This distinction is important to understand. High-volume/low-dollar organizations use broadbased solicitation methods to acquire many small- to mid-sized gifts. These organizations are very successful in reaching donors who make decisions based on their income. In contrast, high-dollar/low-volume organizations use high-touch methods of personal relationship building to acquire relatively few very large gifts. Asset wealth drives these very large gifts.

When donors receive a direct mail appeal, an e-mail appeal, or a phone solicitation, they likely ask themselves, "What can I afford to give?" or "What is in my budget for charity?" This is an income-driven decision process. Charity for these donors, at least in the context of these types of appeals, engages their perceptions of cash flow. Dollar amounts from these types of appeals is generally low- to mid-sized, and it is often assumed that cash flow enables organizations as well as individuals to run.

When donors are solicited after being cultivated by a case for support, they likely ask themselves, "Is this worthy of my investment?" or "Will this organization accomplish this important goal?" This is an asset-driven decision process. Charity in this case bears a closer resemblance to financial investments. These donors look for a return on this investment. The return is not financial; rather, it is the accomplishment of a goal or a realization of a vision. Large sums of capital dollars are needed by start-up companies to launch new products or by real estate professionals to construct a new residential development. Likewise, in philanthropy, asset-based gifts are perceived to change, build, or transform an organization.

New prospect researchers often make certain assumptions about potential prospects. For example, they might mention they scoured their database for lawyers, doctors, and chief executives. Law and medicine tend often to be high-income, low-asset fields. They earn at a high level, but they are still among the income class. Chief executives may have substantial stock wealth or ownership in a company, but often they are at the high end of the income class as well.

Seasoned prospect researchers have seen the kind of prospects who travel through the cultivation process and give major gifts. These researchers have met with many gift officers and have seen which prospects turn out to be the best donors. They will more likely scour the database for business owners, entrepreneurs, and real estate investors. These groups may not have obvious cash flow, but they are quite accustomed to the concepts of start-up capital, financial capital, and cultivating partners for large projects. The daily work of these types of donors largely mimics the same thought process as consideration of giving substantial philanthropic gifts.

For donors from these segments, nonprofits need to make the following case:

- The project is important.
- This project aligns with the donor's value portfolio.
- The organization will deliver on this project.
- The donor will get a return on his/her investment.

This is a very different message than the one often seen in broadbased appeals. Also, it steps away from the give-back messages often seen in higher education. It presents a "give-forward" message critical to high-dollar gifts. Although the most efficient campaigns are generally driven by these very large gifts from the top 1% of the database, many high-volume organizations are very effective fundraisers. Nonetheless, the trend in fundraising organizations is to convert to this high-dollar approach.

Avoiding need-based messages is almost a cliché in fundraising literature. The negative impact of need-based messaging on production can be dramatic. Anecdotally, many fundraising professionals have observed this phenomenon. Often there can be short-term successes, but these are followed by marked declines. Understanding cash flow versus investment is the key to knowing why need-based messages fail in the long term. Imagine a retailer making this pitch:

"Our sales in this quarter were down, we are laying off 10% of our work force, we are closing 25 stores, and we lost our CEO to the competitor. Because of our challenges, we really need you to step forward and invest in our stock."

How do you think that would work? Similarly, for a major donor who is investing in your program, the following message will also fail:

"Our organization is facing a time of financial tribulation. Our key donor has reduced his annual commitment. We have had to scale back on some key programs. To move forward, we are counting on your philanthropic support."

It seems almost comical, but I see these kinds of messages regularly at many struggling organizations.

Philanthropic Motivations

If giving were just a question of assets and income, fundraising would be easy. But as we all know, it is more complicated than financials. Throughout my study of fundraising, the question I have found the most interesting is, "Why do people give?" If we are in the business of receiving gifts, this should be a question we all ask. From my research, I have segmented the motivations for giving into five primary types:

1. Loyalty
2. Global impact
3. Personal interest
4. Duty
5. Empathy

Loyalty   Loyalty as a motivation is generally earned by an organization. In for-profit companies, loyalty is achieved by consistently meeting needs. For example, when most people make travel plans, they look for cost first. If I am flying to Los Angeles, I might look at Southwest, Northwest, Continental, and so on until I found the best price. Let's say I chose Northwest in this case and had a positive flying experience. I would remember this. Now, say I am flying to New York and I go through the list again. This time, I choose Northwest again and have another positive experience. Up to this point the airlines have been a conduit for my need of traveling to a destination. Eventually, I might get to the point of going directly to the Northwest Airlines Web site without checking the others. Northwest consistently met my needs and built loyalty. My choice now includes the airline as well as the travel goal.

Now let's say I have an interest in theater. In the Minneapolis area, we have many fine theater companies, so I have many choices. Let's say I give gifts to the Guthrie Theater, Theatre de la Jeune Lune, and the theater program at the University of Minnesota, because I am excited about the programming. Imagine that all three acknowledge and thank me for my gift. However, the University consistently points out the impact of my gifts on these programs. Eventually, I may give a gift to the University without seeing the programs for the next season. I have a trust that the program will meet my needs.

Some organizations achieve donor loyalty more quickly than others. Often, they have built a national reputation of consistently achieving goals. In some prestigious universities, loyalty was built while an alumnus was still a student. Regardless of the reputation of an organization, the population of loyalty donors is declining. Because of competition for the philanthropic dollar, organizations need to make extra efforts to communicate impact and success directly resulting from gifts.

Global Impact   Many donors and a large percentage of major philanthropists are motivated by the global impact of a program. Let's say a wealthy individual wanted to see cancer eliminated for the betterment of society. They might choose to give to Memorial Sloan-Kettering, the American Cancer Society, MD Anderson, or any of the other very fine cancer research organizations. The motivation for the gift is the elimination of cancer. The motivation is not Memorial Sloan-Kettering, the American Cancer Society, MD Anderson, or any of the other cancer research organizations. These organizations are vessels between a donor and their interest in the elimination of cancer.

When an investor buys a stock, it is unlikely they do so to make the company better. Rather, their goal is to enjoy a financial return on the investment. For a global impact donor, it is unlikely they give to make a nonprofit better. Rather, their goal is to see a return on their global investment. Again, they are not feeding their financial portfolio, but their value portfolio. Global impact donors need the most strategic cultivation, with donor-relation plans circling back to their goals.

As philanthropic competition increases and loyal donors decrease, the number of philanthropists motivated by global impact grows considerably—

especially at the high levels of the gift pyramid. For high-dollar fundraising organizations, understanding this segment is critical for success.

Personal Interest Donors who give for personal interests are very similar to global impact donors. They also see nonprofits as vessels between their values and their realization. However, the realization is at the local level. I find this group especially prevalent in arts donors. You may hear them say, "We need a thriving arts community in our city." However, this statement is still part of the vessel. Their goal is to have the arts experiences at the personal level made possible by this thriving arts community.

Personally, I am a fan of classical music. My very favorite genre is sacred choral music such as the music of Bach or Mendelssohn. I can think of nothing better than attending a performance of Bach's *St. John's Passion* or Mendelssohn's oratorio, *Elijah*. If I gave to a local orchestra, choral organization, or Bach society, I might believe at one level that the Twin Cities needs a thriving classical music scene. Although this may be true, it is more fully motivated by my interest in experiencing the classical music (Exhibit 2.1).

Duty Another segment of donors gives out of a sense of duty. This population is most often found in religious organizations. Many faith systems have expectations of charity. Although it is expected that concepts such as the tithe are directed towards only religious organizations, many devout individuals view giving a percentage to charity in general as fulfilling this tithing requirement. Even outside of the faith community,

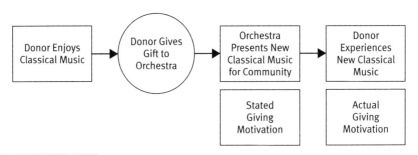

| EXHIBIT 2.1 | **STATED VERSUS ACTUAL GIVING MOTIVATIONS** |

some wealthy individuals feel their financial success obligates them to give to others.

Although duty may personally motivate an individual to give, organizations generally struggle when they use this message. These messages are often put forward by public broadcasting organizations. I will often hear, "If you listen to us everyday, it is your obligation to give to us." There may be a small segment that responds to this message. However, if you are trying to communicate with a loyalty, global impact, or personal interest donor, your message will not resonate. To the loyal donor, it sounds like a spoiled child saying "you owe me dessert after my meal." To the global impact and personal interest donors, you sound like a company saying, "You shop in our stores, it is your obligation to buy our stock."

An organization is best served by leaving the feelings of obligation to the donor. The only successful methods for increasing dollars from this segment involve making it easier to meet these obligations. EFT, or electronic funds transfer, enables a donor to meet their obligations without worrying about it. A high correlation of duty-motivated donors are interested in giving in this way.

Empathy   Many donors give out of a broader sense of empathy for others. Although donors at all levels may give in this way, it is usually low- to mid-range donors who give for these reasons. Donors who step up at times of crisis after disasters such as Hurricane Katrina or the 2004 tsunami are likely to feel the pain of the victims. Rarely does an organization see these donors give regularly or ascend through the gift levels. Also, they often give to many different organizations as the need arises.

These donors will respond to very emotionally presented messages in direct marketing appeals. Measuring response to these appeals in combination with surveys and other philanthropy data enables the identification of these individuals. High-volume children's hospitals may acquire these donors better than most. However, these same organizations have difficulty building major gift programs on this base, since these constituents rarely have investment mentalities.

CLUSTER ANALYSIS CASE STUDY

An effective way to discover naturally occurring segments in your database is to run a cluster analysis. By entering giving information and constituent attributes into a common statistics package, you can group individuals and corporations in ways that might not be obvious to you, yet is obvious to your computer.

Here is a case study of a cluster built recently for a seminary. The goal of the project was to determine the core behavioral groups at this religious institution. Essentially, they wanted to know, "Who is giving to us?" Then, after identifying the clusters, they could follow with custom research and messaging strategies to optimize their major, planned, and annual giving programs.

Method

The first step was to gather a comprehensive query of data, including giving information, geographic distribution, wealth indicators, activities, and demographic attributes. In Chapter 7, the process of selecting a data file is described in depth. The data for modeling was prepared by converting many of the text fields into numeric flags and splitting apart complex variables into smaller pieces. Then the data was entered into a two-step cluster module on SPSS (Statistical Package for the Social Sciences). Several clusters were run until a good separation was found between the groups, with a good variety of characteristics informing the segmentation. After the clusters were built, they were compared to giving and demographic data to produce descriptive summaries of the clusters.

Clusters

This organization had six primary clusters. After conducting some descriptive analysis of their characteristics, they were named to ease explanations. Using terms like "cluster #1" and "cluster #2" will only present confusion in implementation. The names chosen were as follows:

1. Wave Makers
2. Meeting Potential
3. Foundation Builders
4. Low Likelihood Middle (LLM)
5. Hesitant Potential
6. Nonparticipants

Wave Makers   The Wave Makers were the segment leading in all giving measures, including outright as well as planned giving. They had by far the highest giving capacity. Even though Wave Makers represented just shy of 7% of the entire database, they produced 70% of the giving in the seminary's history. As with most models, this cluster was not entirely constructed of top donors. It also contained many individuals who matched other characteristics of the top donors. This group had the best likelihood of making the biggest giving waves in the near future of the seminary.

Meeting Potential   The second-best giving group was the Meeting Potential segment. They did not have the capacity or giving likelihood of the Wave Maker segment. However, this group had shown rapid giving increase in recent years. On average, they were by far the oldest segment, with an average age of 82 years old. Their participation was above average, with giving levels of three to four times the amount of their first gifts. With their modest capacity, they were approaching their giving potential and would not ascend to the major gift level unless new wealth information is discovered.

Foundation Builders   A very prominent and attached segment for the seminary was the Foundation Builders cluster. Except for the Wave Makers, this segment was the highest performing on measurements of participation and giving planned gifts. However, this segment also had the lowest levels of capacity and likelihood measurements for major gifts. An interesting fact about the segment was the total inclusion of the alumni. They would continue to be very loyal to the seminary but did not have the means to make outright transforming gifts unless they lay the foundation through deferred means.

Low Likelihood Middle (LLM)   A segment of mid-range donors had low likelihoods for participation and gave rather sporadically. They had some financial potential but relatively cold relationships with the seminary. This group could be warmed through annual giving and event strategies. Unless new information is learned or the relationship was warmed, it did not make sense to allocate major gift officer resources to this group.

Hesitant Potential   A slightly wealthier, yet unconvinced group was the Hesitant Potential cluster. They were "dabblers" in their giving. Dabbling is a common characteristic of wealthy donors. If a relationship could be built and the assets were there, they could be converted to Wave Makers in the future. However, the Wave Makers had a higher current likelihood for major giving. For this type of segment, I would hold off on assigning major giving officers until the relationship solidifies. Natural peers and volunteers may be a key for engaging this segment.

Nonparticipants   And finally, we identified the segment of Nonparticipants. This segment was roughly 38% of the file. It was made up primarily of non-donors and individuals matching the profile of non-donors. There was minimal data to suggest any relationship or connection. The group was the least likely to respond to any messages or give at any level. For this type of cluster, I would suggest minimizing costs by decreasing the amount of attention paid through all means of activity. Precious resources are better spent on those with a higher likelihood of participating in response to appeals.

Below are a few examples of the differences between the clusters:

Average First Gift by Clusters

	Mean	Median
0 - Nonparticipants	$0.00	$0.00
1 - Meeting Potential	$440.40	$20.00
2 - Foundation Builders	$116.19	$25.00
3 - Low Likelihood Middle	$34.61	$0.00
4 - Wave Makers	$2,036.77	$50.00
5 - Hesitant Potential	$73.64	$0.00

Average Largest Group by Clusters

	Mean	Median
0 - Nonparticipants	$0.00	$0.00
1 - Meeting Potential	$1,413.17	$25.00
2 - Foundation Builders	$578.70	$75.00
3 - Low Likelihood Middle	$40.85	$0.00
4 - Wave Makers	$9,209.34	$100.00
5 - Hesitant Potential	$89.94	$0.00

Average Age (known on only 20% of the database)

	Mean	Median
0 - Nonparticipants	53	50
1 - Meeting Potential	84	87
2 - Foundation Builders	62	61
3 - Low Likelihood Middle	64	64
4 - Wave Makers	76	78
5 - Hesitant Potential	71	71

Frequency of Giving Index

	Mean	Median
0 - Nonparticipants	0.03	0.00
1 - Meeting Potential	1.69	0.00
2 - Foundation Builders	2.64	3.00
3 - Low Likelihood Middle	0.51	0.00
4 - Wave Makers	4.47	5.00
5 - Hesitant Potential	0.87	0.00

Likelihood of Giving Major Gift (0-1000 model, 1000 being the highest)

	Mean	Median
0 - Nonparticipants	257	298
1 - Meeting Potential	724	758
2 - Foundation Builders	575	659
3 - Low Likelihood Middle	626	709
4 - Wave Makers	798	815
5 - Hesitant Potential	611	677

Average Capacity

	Mean	Median
0 - Nonparticipants	$0.00	$0.00
1 - Meeting Potential	$67,815.55	$4,334.90
2 - Foundation Builders	$44,473.91	$4,410.10
3 - Low Likelihood Middle	$73,031.80	$4,800.00
4 - Wave Makers	$1,323,885.04	$5,061.00
5 - Hesitant Potential	$65,914.08	$4,578.60

FINAL THOUGHTS ON UNDERSTANDING YOUR CONSTITUENTS

Throughout this chapter, the importance of understanding not only *who* your constituents are but also *why* they give to you was described. A key component of analytics is using data for understanding. But it is so much more than just knowing facts. The facts help you to see that while there is great diversity among your constituents, there are also commonalities.

By focusing attention on commonalities, large populations can be reached in ways that seem more personal. By understanding why people give gifts to an organization, a better message for mass communications can be developed. When you know which characteristics to research, your prospecting efforts will be more efficient. Organizations will have better success in meeting new donors when qualifying prospects for major giving.

My hope is that the industry moves beyond considering only capacity and likelihood to give and pays considerable attention to giving motivation. Philanthropy is such a rewarding activity for our donors. We can enhance this feeling of pride if we can tap into the values and goals motivating our donors, and our dollars will increase. It's a win–win situation.

CHAPTER 3

Analytics and Prospecting

The leading fundraising nonprofits raise money through a combination of base development and major gift solicitation. The process of moving individuals from the base into the major giving pipeline is called prospecting. For these organizations to be effective in their major gift fundraising, the prospecting program needs to be both productive and efficient.

Data mining is an effective technique for adding both productivity and efficiency to an integrated prospecting system. However, to understand data mining's role, it is important to describe prospecting in the context of the development business process.

DEVELOPMENT BUSINESS PROCESS

Development has three primary elements defining the business process (Exhibit 3.1). These are:

1. *Base development:* Annual giving and membership programs
2. *Prospecting:* Identifying and prioritizing prospects for major giving
3. *Major giving:* Cultivating and stewarding major gifts

Base development is the process of building the base of constituents and engaging them in philanthropic behavior. Annual giving programs serve this purpose for most higher education and health care organizations. Most other nonprofits often have membership programs. Many donors will only ever give to a base development program. Many, however, can and will give at a much higher level if:

- The nonprofit builds institutional loyalty.
- The case for support aligns with the donor's interests.

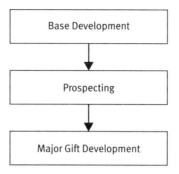

EXHIBIT 3.1   BUSINESS PROCESS FOR DEVELOPMENT

and:

- The donor has the financial capacity to give at the higher level.
- This donor was identified for major giving through prospecting strategies.

Prospecting is the method of finding individuals in the base and feeding them into the major giving pipeline. The techniques used for prospecting are often good indicators of the development sophistication of a nonprofit. Organizations very new or less sophisticated in prospecting rely nearly entirely on gift-based prospecting. More sophisticated programs use an integrated system of market-level research, individual-level research, field discovery, and prospect pool monitoring.

Gift-based prospecting is done by watching gifts as they come in through base development efforts. Once these gifts reach a certain size, the donor is flagged for individual attention. This approach is based on an assumption that donors follow a cycle that mirrors our development process. This giving cycle says that donors give gifts to the base, they become loyal through consistent giving, this giving increases, they transition to major gift levels, and as they approach the ends of their lives, they give planned gifts.

As a data analyst, I have tried to substantiate many of these industry-standard notions. Some I can prove; others I cannot. This cycle of giving is one that I can partially substantiate, but not fully. The donors I described as Loyalty donors in the previous chapter are the only group that seem to follow this progression. A good portion of Duty donors also follow this progression, but the majority of the others do not. Global Impact and

Personal Interest donors who give major gifts most often have unpredictable giving patterns before giving these major gifts. These donors are acquired in the base, but they do not give consistently. There may be years between gifts; increases in giving are sporadic and may spike rather than show gradual inclines. Some may even have their first gifts be at the major level.

Much of the difference between donors with predictable giving patterns versus those with sporadic giving patterns is income versus asset motivation. Those giving out of income are more likely to be scheduled in their giving. Also, they likely maintain a similar percentage of their budget dedicated to charity. As income increases, so does giving. This pattern is more predictable. Asset donors are more likely to test the waters before making an investment. Since the overall driver for giving is confidence, they are testing you to see how the money is spent and how you communicate this back to them.

If this very high level of donors, those giving from assets, is inconsistent in their giving patterns, a gift-based prospecting system will present great opportunity risks. Organizations with this system are just scratching the surface of the gift potential in their base and community. Since previous giving is insufficient in identifying major giving prospects, organizations need to diversify their prospecting efforts.

Let's review why major donors give:

- The nonprofit builds institutional loyalty.
- The case for support aligns with the donor's interests.

and

- The donor has the financial capacity to give at the higher level.
- This donor was identified for major giving through prospecting strategies.

Previous giving might infer institutional loyalty and possibly capacity, but there are other factors that indicate loyalty and capacity. The other motivations need additional sources of information. If we were to summarize these reasons into criteria, they would be called:

- Affinity
- Interests
- Capacity
- Likelihood

Affinity

A person may give to an organization because he or she has an affinity for that organization. Affinity, in this case, is defined as having positive feelings about an institution. Generally, giving affinity comes from earned loyalty. How does an organization earn loyalty?

An MBA student may learn the following equation (Exhibit 3.2).

As an organization continues to meet the needs of a customer, it builds a sense of loyalty in that customer. For example, let's say you are in the market for a new television. Your consumer need is this television. You may shop at Circuit City, Best Buy, Sears, and Ultimate Electronics. Because of your shopping experience, price, location, and product features, you chose to purchase your television at Best Buy. Now imagine you are in the market for a new surround sound system for your television. You may look at the same four retailers this time as well. If, this time, you choose Best Buy again, they met your consumer need again. Eventually, if Best Buy continues to meet your consumer needs, you would make your next purchase at Best Buy without shopping around. They have earned your customer loyalty.

The same premise is true for nonprofit organizations. Both services offered and donor experience can translate into loyalty if the nonprofit consistently delivers. For an arts organization, consistently performed, stellar productions will earn loyalty from people who enjoy performances. For an educational institution, the student and alumni experiences both develop loyalty. For the health care organization, dedicated and service-oriented doctors may develop a loyal patient base. For conservation organizations, demonstrated success in protecting land and wildlife may build loyalty among constituents. For all organizations, having a

EXHIBIT 3.2   **FORMULA FOR CALCULATING CUSTOMER LOYALTY**

positive giving experience from first contact through stewardship can build organizational loyalty.

Interests

In the first chapter, a person's value portfolio was discussed. The value portfolio contains a person's guiding principles and affinities in life, which may be as simple as a hobby or as involved as a life's ambition. I will use myself as an example.

VALUE PORTFOLIO OF JOSHUA BIRKHOLZ

BUSINESS

- Career in nonprofit fundraising
- Progressed from college-based fundraising, through prospect research and management, to data mining at the University of Minnesota, to consulting in prospecting and advancement services, to managing an analytics division at a national fundraising consulting firm in 10 years

Summary: Interested in nonprofits, service and teaching, innovation, and making a contribution to the field.

EDUCATION

- Undergraduate schooling in music
- Graduate work in nonprofit management focusing on the arts, culminating in a master's degree
- Graduate studies in music during employment
- Additional studies in data mining, statistics, and database administration

Summary: Interested in music and nonprofit management. Possibly works long hours, as evidenced by working on a second master's while holding down a full-time job.

PERSONAL

- Married with three young daughters. Wife is a teacher. Children are involved in community arts and athletics programs.

- Father, grandfather, and great-grandfather are all Lutheran ministers.
- Attends father's Lutheran church with wife and kids.

Summary: Strong sense of family and heritage, community, and Lutheranism.

CIVIC

- Former conductor of local Lutheran Chamber Choir
- Former founding board member of international ESL organization
- Former church council/music director positions
- Attends alumni events at private high school

Summary: Interested in church music, international impact, and participating civically.

HOBBIES AND ENTERTAINMENT

- Composing music
- Watching movies at home
- Watching Twins baseball games with the family

Summary: Activities involving music or family

KEY ELEMENTS

- Success for nonprofits
- Service- and teaching-oriented
- Innovation
- Personal impact on field and world
- Interest in music
- Hard working
- Family and heritage
- Community services
- Lutheranism
- Participation

VALUE SUMMARY

Joshua Birkholz values his personal innovation and impact on the world through helping nonprofits, volunteering for international causes, and working tirelessly in a professional service industry. He values faith, family, and his roots. He maintains an active interest in music, especially choral and church music.

After this summary of interests, listed below are some of the organizations I've given to over these years:

- University of Minnesota School of Music
- Friends of China, an international ESL organization
- Kingdom Workers, a Lutheran local and international service organization
- The Cantabilé Singers, a Minneapolis area chamber choir
- Local Lutheran congregation and synod

Do these organizations fit my value portfolio? Do you know how to communicate your mission to align it with a giving prospect's interests?

Capacity

Let's face it, major gifts come from wealthy people. Every prospecting program should be able to rank the entire database by financial capacity to give. They can't afford not to. Many of my clients have individual donors that out-give their entire annual fund programs. How much do you spend on your direct mail campaign? Now, how much do you spend on wealth data acquisition?

I heard the economist Steven Levitt speak in fall 2007. As he was discussing some of his consulting with businesses, he said one thing that stuck with me. The comment was along the lines of, "For almost every company, I tell them they are underpriced."

As a fundraising consultant, I can safely say, "For almost every development program, I tell them they are under-asking." Nine times out of ten this is true.

Organizations set different levels for major giving. The most common is $25,000 in a 5-year pledge or more. With a salary of $50,000 annually, a person could be a major donor by giving 10% annually. Obviously, it depends on the organization being the sole recipient of this person's charitable giving. This fact should elicit the following responses:

- With increasing salaries, the majority of our constituents are capable of giving major gifts.
- How do we become a top giving recipient for our constituents?
- Should we increase our major giving level to focus on the true top of the pyramid?

It should be the goal of every prospecting program to know which prospects have the most financial capacity. And it should be the responsibility of every major giving program to ensure that all of these prospects are managed, cultivated, and solicited appropriately. Often, I see high-level prospects ignored for the sake of lower-level prospects with longer relationships. As a matter of organizational stewardship, the top prospects should be in the portfolios of major gift officers.

Likelihood

Although all major donors are wealthy, not all wealthy people will be your major donors. It can be tempting to add records into your database for every wealthy individual, even if there is no connection to your organization or alignment with your mission. Although you can build a connection, it is important to understand which prospects are already close to you or in alignment. Part of prospecting is prioritizing donors, and understanding which donors are currently most likely to give is a key indicator of priority.

There are many ways to measure likelihood or propensity to give. The most common is a qualitative assessment made by a major giving officer after meeting and interacting with the prospect. Some prospect research departments make qualitative assessments based on an interpretation of information gathered through online and printed resources. Certainly, previous giving indicates a propensity to give, as this behavior is demonstrated.

Many prospecting strategies revolve around giving or capacity as an initial filter of the base, but identifying areas such as likelihood, affinity, and interests are generally left to case-by-case research or field qualification work.

INTEGRATED PROSPECTING SYSTEM

Building the most efficient and productive prospecting systems requires diverse approaches to understanding all criteria at all stages of identification. From initial market research techniques filtering the base, to one-to-one prospect research techniques, to gift officer field qualification, it is wise to consider affinity, interests, capacity, and likelihood (Exhibit 3.3).

One way to think about prospecting is as a system of risk management. For an organization to provide individual attention to high-level prospects, the organization must pay the salary, travel, and working expenses of the gift officers. Add to this the short supply of strong fundraising talent, the

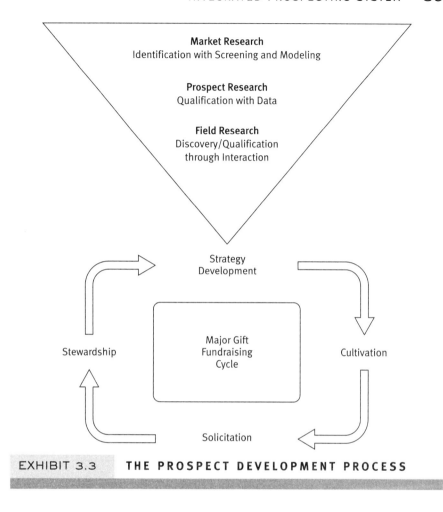

EXHIBIT 3.3   THE PROSPECT DEVELOPMENT PROCESS

high turnover facing organizations, and average ramp-up periods of two or more years for these field officers, and you begin to see that it requires a substantial investment to deploy field officers, not to mention supporting this group with an adequate infrastructure. Many nonprofits have too few staff for the potential in their database and a limited ability for expansion. Assigning gift officers to prospects other than those with the most financial capacity and likelihood to give presents substantial risk to an organization.

Another area of risk is the solicitation process. Asking a prospect for less than their capacity at the wrong time or for the wrong project can cost organizations money. If a gift officer asks a prospect with a capacity of more than $1 million for $100,000, it costs the nonprofit $900,000 in opportunity.

When a gift officer goes into the field to qualify a new prospect, the cost of this work should be considered, too. Imagine half a day's salary, travel costs (additional if air travel is required), meal costs, etc. Sending a representative to qualify new prospects will cost thousands of dollars. If they were to see names that never made their way into the cultivation process, how much did that cost? There is a risk to not prequalifying these names before the visit.

Prospect research is not a free activity, either. Salary costs, subscription resources, and limited time must be considered. How much does it cost to research a name that will never move into the discovery process? Often-quoted industry standards dictate goals of three suspects for every prospect. Many researchers will log six or seven names researched for each name qualified in the field. With average qualification times of 60 to 75 minutes per suspect, it takes a full day's work to find one person. How would an organization benefit from finding two per day?

Finally, when prospects enter the cultivation process, there is a risk of prospects slipping through the cracks. A full-time gift officer who can make 20 visits in a month, which is an industry standard yet rarely achieved goal, would have 240 visits in a year. Considering holidays, vacations, events, and other duties, 200 visits is an aggressive yearly goal. Now, if an average gift requires a discovery visit, three cultivation visits, a solicitation visit, and a return visit to steward the gift, it takes six visits to maintain a relationship with one prospect. (It generally takes seven or eight visits per gift rather than this standard six.) But, even using six visits per prospect, a gift officer can manage relationships with 100 prospects, or 166 in a 5-year period. The standard portfolio size in fundraising is 150 to 175 prospects, based on this logic.

How many gift officers maintain portfolios exceeding 175 names? Can they maintain relationships with all of these prospects? Considering that most major giving programs stop or decrease broadbased solicitations to assigned prospects, what does it cost to not maintain the relationship with the prospect? If prospects slip through the cracks and are not moved through to solicitation, what does that cost an organization?

The six areas of prospecting risk described above are:

1. Managing low-level prospects at the expense of high-level prospects
2. Inappropriate solicitation

3. Inefficient deployment of field staff
4. Inefficient research qualification
5. Oversized portfolios
6. Letting prospects slip through the cracks

All of these areas of risk are managed by developing an integrated prospecting system. By assessing, maintaining, and monitoring prospects according to capacity and likelihood indicators, the prospecting program makes sure the best prospects are always given the attention they deserve. High-level individual research, including detailed capacity estimates, manages the risk of inappropriate solicitation. Prospect research qualification reduces risk for deploying gift officers into the field. Advanced filtering techniques, such as screening, surveys, and data mining, prequalify names to manage inefficiencies in prospect research. Prospect tracking systems with dedicated staffing ensure portfolio sizes are appropriate and prospects are given the attention they need.

In larger organizations, it is common to see various departments within prospecting or prospect research dedicated to these various areas of process management. Some of these departments include the traditional request and profile researchers, the prospect identification specialists, data analysis and modeling specialists, and a dedicated prospect management team.

In smaller organizations, these same areas are represented by one or two prospecting staff. A director of research may manage screening and data mining projects while coordinating with the field team on prospect management issues. An associate may field requests, qualify new names,

Areas of Risk	Prospecting Program Solution
Managing low-level prospects at the expense of high-level prospects	Portfolio analysis and maintenance
Inappropriate solicitation	Prospect research profiling
Inefficient deployment of field staff	Prospect research qualification
Inefficient research qualification	Market research (screening, surveys, data mining)
Oversized portfolios	Prospect management and tracking program
Letting prospects slip through the cracks	Prospect management and tracking program

and conduct more detailed research on prospects nearing solicitation. Additionally, this division of activities may correspond with the campaign period. Early in a campaign, the prospecting staff may focus on market research projects, prospect identification, and portfolio clean-up activities. Later in the campaign, the focus may be on aggressive prospect management and solicitation support.

ANALYTICS AS PART OF THE PROSPECTING SYSTEM

Traditional prospect research programs grew out of a support need for the cultivation and solicitation process. Early researchers frequented libraries and file rooms to gather information. The Internet made their work much more efficient and productive. After organizations became more sophisticated and exhausted the self-identifying prospects, researchers needed to develop prospect identification strategies. They began by reviewing lists of names from published resources and previous donors by volunteers and top donors. News alert services and database screening made this work much more efficient and productive. In the past 15 years, the industry saw a rapid period of database conversion. The database was no longer just a gift accounting system. Prospect researchers and fundraisers used the database to store biographical, transactional, and relationship data about their constituents. Annual giving and membership programs stored appeal history. Alumni relations and events departments stored participation data.

Now, these very sophisticated systems have produced a nagging feeling of missed opportunity. We see these great quantities of multidimensional data points, and we are not tapping them. This feeling of untapped potential has driven the rise in many industries for analytics. By tapping into this data, we are more productive in identifying prospects, more accurate in our mass solicitations, and more efficient in our processes.

In prospecting, analytics are most often applied to inform the composition of gift officer portfolios and identify new prospects by statistical likelihood of giving major and planned gifts.

Portfolio Composition

After conducting constituency analysis projects like those described in Chapter 2, it is a helpful exercise to understand the breakdown of segments within the portfolio. You will notice some gift officers lean towards managing constituents with specific characteristics. You will see some that close gifts with one segment very well but not with others. And you will see some segments outperform the others across the board.

In analyzing and populating portfolios, the goals should be twofold:

1. Place the right prospects with the right gift officers
2. Optimize distribution of constituents to maximize yield

If a gift officer is very successful producing gifts from certain demographic or industry segments, it is likely that he or she will continue to be successful with those groups. The best prospects for a gift officer are the ones that enable him or her to be the most successful.

As you assess prospects' capacity and likelihood of giving, you will notice that certain combinations of ratings will also out-give other combinations. The perfect prospect is the one with high capacity to give and a high likelihood to give a major gift. However, there may be relatively few of these. Some constituents have high capacity with low likelihoods of giving. The populations need more cultivation before giving. Other prospects have high likelihoods of giving gifts to you, but they lack the capacity. These might be better allocated to leadership of annual giving programs to sustain the relationship. They might also be given to planned giving programs to use creative means of giving larger gifts.

Some gift officers take longer to cultivate major gifts than other officers. Others are very quick to solicit. Those who take too long with a constituent who is ready to give run the risk of wearing out the sentiment of giving. Those who ask prematurely of constituents with colder relationships risk pushing a prospect away altogether. One way to optimize the portfolio is to align average cultivation timelines of gift officers to the readiness for solicitation of prospects. It might be perfectly fine to have some gift officers specializing in short-term cultivation projects and others specializing in warming cold relationships. Segmenting in this way may yield a higher result.

Another way of optimizing portfolios is determining the perfect balance of constituency segments and ratings combinations to maximize the yields of the portfolios. This is very similar to diversifying a stock portfolio. The constituency segments might be a rough equivalent of the industries of public companies. The ratings combinations might be a rough equivalent of return and risk.

Predicting Major Giving

The most common ways of predicting major giving in this industry are by ranking correlated factors and using regression analysis. Both techniques are described in the *how-to* chapters later in the book.

Correlation In comparing certain data points to each other, such as giving and age, you may notice that some move together and others do not. For example, if age goes up, giving goes up; these variables might be said to move together. Some variables move in opposite directions—for example, as the number of late payments goes up, the credit score goes down. Other data points may have no relationship at all. For example, the number of square feet in the library and the percentage of people in a community who use the library. Even data points that seem to have no correlation may turn out to have a correlation if one introduces a factor such as the population of the community.

These examples describe the relationship between two points. This is called correlation. Correlation does not mean that one causes the other; rather, it only shows that they move together. Of the examples above, the credit score example might be the only one where causality might be proved. This is because payment history is a component of the credit score.

If you were to change attributes to numbers, you could measure them using correlation. Let's say we tracked members of the alumni association. We could make a variable where one equaled yes and zero equaled no. We could describe the movement as going from "not a part of the alumni association" to "being a part of the alumni association." Then we could measure it against giving. We might see that the two variables move together.

If you were to transform several of these characteristics into numbers, you could identify 10 or 15 characteristics with strong correlations to major giving. Many organizations will identify these characteristics and combine them into a simple ranking score. If a person has one of the characteristics, they get one point. If they have two characteristics, they get two points. And it continues up to a score of 10 or 15 points. This score will likely be more correlated to major giving than any single factor by itself.

After following this process, the idea is to review those with high scores who are not already major donors. In most cases, they will have a higher likelihood of giving a major gift than those with lower rankings.

Regression Analysis   Imagine you had a giant magician hat. In that hat, let's say there are 500 slips of paper folded in half. Written on 50 slips of the paper are the words, "Major Donor." If you were to cover your eyes and randomly grab slips of paper, you are likely to pull one major donor for every ten draws on average.

Now, let's say that there are several other characteristics of these slips of paper independent of them saying "Major Donor." Perhaps some of the slips of paper are in various shapes like circles, squares, or stars. Let's say some of the slips of paper are very large, some are medium-sized, and others are very small. Let's also say some of these slips are red, some are blue, and others are yellow.

Now, this time we will draw 100 slips of paper out of the hat and record these various independent characteristics as well as whether or not the slip was a major donor. After pulling the slips of paper we might notice that five of the ten major donor slips were red slips of paper. Based on this information alone, we might be tempted to look for more red slips of paper to find more major donors. However, we have not looked at the other 90 yet. What if 45 of those 90 slips were also red? That would mean that 50 percent of the major donors are red and 50 percent of the non-major donors are red.

This is an important thing to understand. So many fundraising organizations will send surveys to the major donors annually. Then, based on the responses to those surveys, they will plan their prospecting strategies. What they failed to do was observe those same responses in the random populations of their databases. For example, let's say in a recent survey, 70% of major donors said that they were married. The prospecting department may pull a list from the database using marital status as a criteria. Now let's say that 70% of the entire database was married. In this case, knowing someone is married does not increase the odds of finding a major donor. Now let's say that only 15% of the major donors said they owned their own business. Based on this number alone, a prospecting program may not look for business owners. However, what if only 1% of the entire database owned their own companies? Now we have a characteristic that dramatically increases our odds of finding a major donor.

Sometimes when you combine characteristics, the relationship changes. For example, what if 30% of the major donor slips were blue, while 20%

of the random population was blue. And, let's say 40% of the major donors were square-shaped, while only 20% of the random population was square-shaped. Both blue and square would be correlated with major giving. But what if only 20% of the major donors were both blue and square, and 20% of the random population were both blue and square? There would be no relationship. In a ranking of correlation, one point would be a stronger indicator of major giving than two points.

Because variables sometimes show reverse effects when combined, some correlations are greater than others, and when you add characteristics together and fewer and fewer cases have all of the characteristics, there are significant limitations to ranking systems based only on correlation. A method of dealing with these characteristics is called regression analysis. Regression analysis observes all of these characteristics (shapes, color, size) that are independent of the slips saying "major donor" and produces a formula weighting each of the characteristics as they relate to "major donor" and as they interact with each other.

Basically, in regression, the computer looks in the hat for the best number of blues, reds, yellows, squares, circles, stars, larges, mediums, and smalls to increase the odds of pulling out a major donor.

In predicting major giving, you would mark all your records that are major donors. Next, you would place all of your records or a random sample of your records into your hat called "statistics software." These records would also have many of these characteristics you converted into numbers. Then the software would find the perfect combination of characteristics to increase your odds of selecting major donors from your file. After finding this combination, it can create a probability score. Similar to ranking systems, those with high probabilities who are not yet major donors would most likely *be* major donors, according to the formula.

Additional Applications of Analytics

The most common application of analytics for prospecting is the prospect identification model outlined above. This looks at current major or planned donors and finds those common characteristics to help identify new leads. Prospecting programs at some institutions also use analytics for other purposes. Some of these include:

- Using text mining to assign group memberships
- Using composite scoring to integrate multiple ratings and indicators
- Leveraging survey data

Using Text Mining to Assign Group Memberships   Text mining is a method of extracting value from free text data. Many large-scale survey researchers will search for common phrases and terms in free text responses to measure against behaviors. There are very few organizations using this text-mining process for prospect identification. The primary reason is the nature of the fundraising database. The only records that generally have free text information are currently identified major donors and prospects. This is because the most common free text fields are the contact report and prospect research information. Contact reports are filed by major giving officers to capture the details of recent interactions. Prospect research does not gather information on individuals unless they are already identified as potential leads. Just the presence of free text data would identify existing constituents already known to the major giving program.

However, within this pool of prospects, text data can be helpful for assigning group memberships. Part of prospecting is identifying prospects overall. Another part is developing groups or pools for special initiatives. Text string analysis could be used in models predicting scholarship giving, library giving, athletics, and other areas. For the scholarship model, phrases such as, "accessibility for students," "make it easier for students," "scholarship," "pay for school," "the cost of education," and so forth could be pulled. These phrases in contact reports and research material were strongly correlated with scholarship giving and they were known prospects. In this case, text mining helped determine which campaign initiative was the best fit.

Using Composite Scoring to Integrate Multiple Ratings and Indicators   I had one client ask me to help with a unique situation. This organization had numerous screening projects, ratings from several staff members, targeting data, wealth data from prospect research, and giving histories. As they tried to prioritize the data and feed the campaign pyramid, they were spinning their wheels on an oil slick of ratings. They asked me to take all of their information and create one ranking incorporating all of it.

This is a relatively easy thing to do when armed with analytics firepower. We loaded all of the information into one master file. We scrubbed bad data and normalized all of the ratings into numeric formats. For example, we took the bottom end of capacity ranges, converted alphanumeric codes to the dollars they represented, and so forth. Then we applied the same capacity formula used by researchers to derive capacity ratings from all of the separate asset data. After doing this, we took the maximum values and minimum values for all of the ratings. We did random hand-verification to determine how close the derived capacity was to a hand-qualified capacity. Then we ranked the entire database from beginning to the end. We produced distinct rankings much like college football rankings. They had their number one prospect, number two prospect, number 3,742 prospect, and so on. And we had one capacity rating for filling the gift pyramid.

Leveraging Survey Data As organizations continue to build their analytics capacity, they find themselves increasing the frequency with which they conduct survey projects. The most common projects focus on understanding constituency profiles and identifying prospects. When conducting clustering projects, as described in Chapter 2, a common follow-up is to survey the clusters. Let's say, based on cluster analysis, that you theorized you had the following four primary groups in your major donor prospect pool:

1. Entrepreneurs
2. Lifelong savers
3. Large company executives
4. Trust fund babies

You might follow this theory by constructing a survey or interviews. Each of the questions is oriented on the characteristics of the clusters. For example, you might ask questions about saving money, investing aggressively, not investing at all, or relying on a company 401(k). Or maybe you ask about using financial advisors, learning from parents, and so on. The idea of the study is to reveal which of the four groups best fits the survey responder.

The challenge with surveys is the limited response. Not everyone will fill out the survey. However, using regression analysis, you can gather all of the people that fit the entrepreneur category and code them on your database. Then you can run a regression analysis to find other people that "look like" the entrepreneurs, even though they did not fill out a survey. You may also use discriminant analysis to run all four categories at once. Analytics enables you to expand the reach of your survey.

Case Story: Analytics and Prospecting

In the past year, I was working with a children's hospital as it was building its capacity for analytics. Their goal was to build a model for predicting major giving, but they wanted to do it themselves rather than outsource the work. I worked with their database administrator, who had a thousand and one other responsibilities. Still, after just a few days of working with statistics software, he was able to build a strong regression model predicting giving to the children's hospital.

Here was the process we followed to build this model:

1. We discussed a business model for data mining to understand why we were doing it, what we hoped to accomplish, and how we knew if we would be successful.
2. We reviewed all of the available data, including giving history, patient data (within HIPAA compliance), activities, demographics, and geography.
3. We extracted this data from the database in a flat comma-delimited format.
4. We imported the data into SPSS software to convert data into numbers and restructure complex variables into smaller pieces.
5. We studied the file and observed the independent correlations between the characteristics and major giving.
6. We produced a model using regression analysis (binary logistic) to predict giving.
7. Finally, we gave every record on their database a score, ranking their position in the model.

After I left, he repeated the process by building his own model predicting planned giving. Now, this children's hospital uses their analytics capacity to feed their prospect research program with new names to qualify for major and planned giving, and they are equipped with better tools for segmenting their direct mail program.

I am continually impressed by how accessible statistics has become. In a relatively short period of time, you can learn how to do calculations that took advanced statistics degrees to accomplish not that long ago.

FINAL THOUGHTS ON ANALYTICS AND PROSPECTING

I started the book by describing how our industry is transforming because our donors are evolving. Philanthropy has become a sophisticated activity. Donors are much more purposeful in their giving and selective about their charities. Prospecting needs to evolve right along with them.

Modern prospecting is much more driven by the values and expectations of the donor. To identify the best prospects for our organization, we need to view it from the donors' perspective: "What is the best organization for me as a prospect?" This means aligning our services with their interests. If they don't match, we move on.

On a small scale, we have been able to do this for some time. We could meet with donors one-on-one and realize when it was not a good fit. Sometimes, we could discover in prospect research when it wasn't a match. However, we were always limited in the filtering process. Analytics equips us to identify a fit between organization and prospect at a much larger scale. It makes our major giving programs more efficient and effective. And, more importantly, we are better serving our donors.

CHAPTER 4

Analytics and Campaign Planning

In modern major gift fundraising, the prevailing model is the five- to seven-year campaign. These comprehensive organizational initiatives furnish opportunities to focus efforts to the greatest areas of opportunity and need, refine the case for support, engage the donor base and top prospects, build internal capabilities, and realize transformational growth. In recent years, the dollar goals have risen exponentially. In some ways, these growing totals reflect healthy competition between organizational peers. At the same time, they challenge development offices and volunteers as they push the boundaries of feasibility.

In assessing the feasibility of a campaign, the fundraising leadership and counsel assess the willingness and ability of the top prospects, the sentiments of the base, the clarity of strategic planning, and the readiness of the organization and its infrastructure. Certainly, within these broad categories are many specifics, such as volunteer engagement, base participation, staff capabilities, leadership strengths, and so on. But overall, the idea is the funding potential of the constituency, strategy, and execution.

For the first one or two campaigns, if the goals are within reason and the organization has some fundraising maturity, these elements often fall into place. There is a group of easily identified prospects within the volunteer core, areas of needs reflect institutional strategic planning, and the infrastructure to research existing prospects, receive gifts, and track contact management may be working and in place. As organizations move from eight-figure campaigns into nine-, ten- and even eleven-figure campaigns, these areas require more effort. The loyal, consistent, and self-identifying donors are not sufficient for reaching the total. Opportunities must engage a broader constituency. Strategies must be in place for all major donor prospects. The infrastructure must support tracking, management, and execution of every level of prospect development, solicitation, and donor relations.

In assessing the feasibility of organizations to undertake campaigns of this magnitude, analytics provide tools to address the additional demands. It provides a means of assessing existing and untapped potential in the constituency. It enables measurement of major donor cultivation strategies. And it guides investments in prospect development and donor relations infrastructure.

ASSESSING CAMPAIGN FACTORS

The criteria reviewed in the prospecting process for assessing potential donors was discussed in Chapter 3. Areas such as capacity, connection, and affinity are considered as the lists are filtered, researched, and qualified for assignment. The same criteria can be used to understand the potential of the entire constituency for campaign planning.

To determine whether a donor is giving to their potential, you must consider their actual giving in relation to their capacity. The capacity rating is a measure of ultimate giving ability over a five-year period. Since this is the case, it is a helpful measurement to compare the capacity rating against the previous five years of giving. Is the donor giving 5% of their potential, 20%, or even 100%? Then consider the entire donor base. What percentage of capacity are donors overall giving to your organization?

To answer this question, you must first develop a composite capacity rating for all records on your database. Similar to assessing individual prospect capacity, you should work from a formula. Variations of the following formula can be used.

Composite Capacity Formula

First, calculate or determine the following:

- Existing capacity rating from the prospect research department
- Existing capacity ratings from screening
- 25% of insider stock holdings (direct holdings and vested options)

- 10% of equity in private companies
- 1% of private company sales, if the individual is a top executive
- 5% of real estate totaling less than $1 million
- 10% of real estate totaling between $1 million and $1.9 million
- 20% of real estate totaling more than $2 million
- 10% of all other identified assets such as art, aircraft, boats, external wealth scores
- 10% of identified income
- 10% of a published net worth amount
- Five times the largest cash gift total in a single fiscal year
- 5% of median income by ZIP code
- 5% of median value of owner-occupied housing by ZIP code

Next, calculate the maximum value from any of the above values. After this calculation, hand-verify the very top values, and smooth them down to account for outliers. For example, you may determine $25 million is the top level a person can get for this composite analysis. If an individual has a higher level, you may change it to $25 million. This cap will vary by organization. Also, at the very top, you are likely to recognize the individuals and may leave them where they are.

If you are after a true aggregate estimate of capacity, the more external data you have, the better. For organizations with very limited screening history, the previous giving estimates may dominate the number. This will make it difficult for determining potential. However, as long as a uniform approach is applied to everybody, you will understand relative performance indicators.

After you determine the composite capacity formula, a series of ratios can be run:

- Capacity yield
- Target efficiency
- Target accuracy
- Close yield

Capacity Yield   Capacity yield is a measurement of the previous five years' giving against the composite capacity score. Calculate this number for everyone, but then look at the average percentages for assigned major gift prospects and all others separately. If you are assessing gift officer performance, it is better to compare the composite capacity to the closed proposal totals.

A common approach to the campaign planning is it takes three prospects for every gift at that level and three suspects for every prospect. If it takes nine individuals with capacity ratings of $1 million to bring in one $1 million gift, the yield would be 11%. As you look at the capacity yield for managed prospects, it is good to see an 11% average as well. If the majority of your capacity ratings are determined by previous giving and not external wealth data, this metric will be artificially high.

At the gift officer level, the capacity yield is an exceptional performance metric. The more seasoned gift officers generally have a higher yield on average within their portfolios. Less experienced gift officers generally have a much smaller yield. Many different factors may cause a small yield. Several of the other ratios listed are used to narrow in on the specific performance gap.

Target Efficiency   The target efficiency metric compares the capacity rating to the target ask amounts. The resulting number informs how a gift officer uses capacity information as they develop their cultivation strategies. Newer gift officers will often see the amount suggested by research and have the following internal dialogue:

> "Prospect research suggested this prospect can give $1 million. How much can we expect to get? Perhaps, $100,000?"

More experienced gift officers will generally see the amount suggested by research and have a different reaction. They will often have the following internal dialogue:

> "Prospect research suggested this prospect can give $1 million. What will it take for us to get $1 million?"

This second thought process is evident among the most successful gift officers in the industry. They understand that major giving is a process of aligning prospect values with the organizational case. They acknowledge that these gifts may happen only when all the stars are in a line. A solid major giving cultivation plan identifies the stars and determines what it will take to align them.

Target efficiency also demonstrates the trust and relationship between the frontlines and the prospecting infrastructure supporting the frontlines.

Recently, I was watching a Minnesota Twins baseball game where the pitcher, Scott Baker, threw a perfect game into the ninth inning. In the post-game interviews, the sportscasters asked him about his pitch selection. He said, "I just threw what [Mike Redmond, the catcher] signaled." The best pitchers will often have a strong level of trust in their catchers. The catchers see the field differently, they study the batters in advance of the games, they see what the batters see behind the plate, and they can feel in their mitt how a pitcher is throwing their fastballs or their breaking balls.

The relationship between prospecting professionals and gift officers can be very similar. The prospect researchers study prospects every day. They evaluate the financial indicators of giving, they observe the strengths of the gift officers, and they make recommendations for giving based on factual information. However, they never throw the pitch (ask for money). The best gift officers have a strong level of trust in their prospecting colleagues.

After reviewing scores of data sets from all nonprofit sectors, this single metric is the most aligned to gift officer maturity. In fact, often times the top-producing gift officers can be identified from this metric alone, even before seeing the dollars raised.

Target Accuracy   As a gift officer approaches the time of solicitation, the most interest is placed in the actual ask amount. For some gift officers, they often make the ask at the actual target amount. For others, this amount will go up or down. As you do projection planning, you must consider the accuracy of the targets. If you have a total of projected asks for the next quarter, it should be qualified by the percent actually asked by each gift officer.

Let's say we have a gift officer named John. On a consistent basis, John maintains target projections on par with the capacity analysis provided by prospect research. However, when he gets to the actual solicitation, he will ask for a smaller amount than he anticipated. Certainly, circumstances will dictate that discounting a target for the solicitation is appropriate to maximize the opportunity for closing any gift at all. But, let's say John consistently discounts his targets by 40%. If he is projecting targets of $2 million for the next quarter, we reasonably expect that he will ask for $1.2 million.

The manager of the major gift team may see John's consistent discounting and decide to work with John on more accurate projections.

This is an appropriate management response to the situation. The appropriate analytics professional response is different. The goal in reporting a pipeline projecting campaign revenue is accuracy. Until John's target accuracy shows substantial improvement, the appropriate action is to discount the pipeline when making gift projection reports.

Close Yield   Some fundraisers will build strong cultivation strategies with appropriate targets and will ask at the amount they project, but the final gift amount shows a decrease or an increase from the target. This is a measurement of close yields. For many gift officers, this can be the most challenging portion of the solicitation process. After they submit a proposal for a major gift, the follow-up communications suffer, and they are unable to close the deal. For some, it is a symptom of being over-aggressive in getting to the proposal stage without a plan for post-proposal communications. For others, the proposal was premature or even long overdue. In any case, you may see a decline or increase on average between the ask amount and the actual gift in the door. As with the other metrics, this discounting percentage should be considered as you build your pipeline reports.

Gift-Based Projections

By incorporating the analysis of the overall database capacity with these ratios, you will be equipped to make some initial assessments of the potential, strategy, and execution of your campaign. However, when making these projections, always consider the past performance in aggregate to set the base of your expectations.

As with many statistics processes, more is usually more. More data and more cases makes for better analysis. When considering giving patterns over time, the same principles hold true. The farther back you go, and the more specific the data, the better your analysis can be. For most organizations, giving patterns change by the campaign, and 10 years of giving data is often more than sufficient.

One approach is to start by pulling the last 10 years of giving by year for all constituents. Taking only hard-credit gift totals for the fiscal year will avoid double counting. When reviewing annual giving performance, pull the data down to the month level. This enables observation of spike periods within the year and shifts in those patterns caused by strategic moves. For an overall campaign analysis, however, yearly totals will approximate sufficiently.

When this data is loaded into statistics software, the total dollars and donors per year can be calculated, and a trend line forecasting to seven years can be predicted. This initial trend line is the rough estimate to use as a starting point.

After building this aggregate projection, split the giving fields into several pieces. Giving at the annual and mid-range levels in aggregate is generally very predictable. Foundation grant support and bequest realizations may also be very predictable and steady for some institutions. Major level and corporate giving are generally more volatile. They go up and down based on many factors. They are very influenced by the turnover and maturity of the major giving staff. Market conditions may rapidly impact major gifts. Organizational scandals and media events may also impact these dollar amounts. Needless to say, the same projection trend line will not fit these steady sources of income as well as the volatile sources of income.

For the steady sources of income, a simple linear or rolling average projection is generally an accurate predictor. You can even do this simply using a trendline chart in Excel. For the volatile sources of income, you can use a logarithmic or polynomial projection, but these will miss the mark if there is a small number of people at the top. However, at an early stage, this amount can be projected separately to estimate high-level gift projection over the five- to seven-year period.

So far, you have an overall estimate of projected giving based on annual totals, an estimate of steady or baseline giving in which you can place a good amount of confidence, and a ballpark figure estimating the more volatile, major, or "growth" income sources.

Capacity Comparison

The next step is to compare these projection estimates to the overall database capacity. You may start by evaluating the previous seven years of production in relation to the capacity. For those prospects under management, perhaps 8% of their aggregate capacity was closed, while 0.5% of the capacity of unmanaged constituents was raised. You may discover that you will need to close 8.5% of the capacity of the managed prospects and 1% of the capacity of unmanaged individuals to achieve the seven-year projection.

After comparing capacity to the projections, consider several capacity-based scenarios. The first scenario is the capacity of the managed prospects versus the top-rated entities. For example, let's say an organization has 1,000 individuals and corporations assigned to prospect managers. The aggregate capacity of these records may be $500 million. If the major gift team on average closes 5% of the capacity of managed prospects in a seven-year period, we might expect them to raise $25 million.

Now, consider that this same organization has individuals and corporations with higher capacity than those assigned. Let's say the aggregate capacity of the top 1,000 records regardless of management status is $650 million. One might estimate this same 5% close ratio could produce $32.5 million. Cleaning the portfolios to represent the apex of the database could be worth $7.5 million.

To be more specific in evaluating the impact of portfolio cleaning, you should take into account the experience of your major gifts team and the attachment of the unmanaged high-capacity records. Typically, it takes three years for a gift officer to ramp-up to full production. Perhaps that 5% represents two very senior gift officers closing 10% of their portfolio capacity and five gift officers closing 3% of their capacity. These five gift officers have an average one or two years' experience. You may estimate that their close percentages will increase. Also, the unmanaged high-capacity records may be the result of new research on connected records, or they may be the result of Bill Gates syndrome. Bill Gates syndrome is the common disorder of putting all high-wealth individuals in your database on the off-chance that they "could" give you a gift. Rather than focusing on individuals with a connection to your organization or mission, the prospecting effort concentrated on wealth in a vacuum. Even though the unmanaged records may have a high level of wealth, the likelihood of closing these gifts remains extremely low.

I will run several scenarios combining portfolio cleaning and increasing close percentages to determine what an organization *could* bring in from the campaign. I will also consider the point of diminishing return for adding major giving staff. If the average gift officer can manage 150 prospects and ramp-up to the average close metrics in three years, I will determine how many managers can be added until the yield on portfolio capacity diminishes below the ability to close gifts and cover the costs of added staff and overhead. Generally, you are limited by a cap on the cost to raise a dollar set by the board. Hopefully, your organization will have some willingness to relax on this metric if a substantial increase in production is possible.

Connection

It is possible to estimate the funding potential of the constituency using the aggregate capacity analysis. But you must also consider how connected this constituency is in your analysis of potential. Most simple ranking systems will be as effective as probability models in early planning stages. As a fundraising statistician, I thoroughly enjoy building these probability models. However, analytics need not be the most sophisticated science to produce value. Here are some sample connection ranking systems you might consider:

Education: Single-Point System

- Alumni: 1 point
- Donor: 1 point
- Gave in last five years: 1 point
- Gave five or more gifts: 1 point
- Managed/Assigned: 1 point
- Researched: 1 point
- Visited: 1 point
- Attended an event: 1 point
- Trustee: 1 point
- Parent: 1 point
- Faculty/Staff: 1 point

Education: Weighted System

- Alumni: 5 points
- Donor: 5 points
- Gift count:
  - 10 or more gifts: 10 points
  - 5 to 9 gifts: 5 points
- Manager: 20 points
- Any board or group membership: 5 points per board/group
- Total contacts $\times$ 3 = points

- Current campaign prospect: 30 points
- Years since last gift:
  - Lowest through 2: 10 points
  - 2.01 through 5: 5 points
  - 5.01 through 10: 2 points

Health Care: Single-Point System

- Patient: 1 point
- Patient family: 1 point
- Donor: 1 point
- Gave in last five years: 1 point
- Gave five or more gifts: 1 point
- Managed/assigned: 1 point
- Researched: 1 point
- Visited: 1 point
- Attended an event: 1 point
- Trustee: 1 point
- MD/Staff: 1 point
- Other health care giving: 1 point

Health Care: Weighted System

- Patient: 5 points
- Patient family: 5 points
- Donor: 5 points
- Gift count:
  - 10 or more gifts: 10 points
  - 5 to 9 gifts: 5 points
- Manager: 20 points
- Any board, support group, or group membership: 5 points per board/group
- Total contacts $\times$ 3 = points
- Current campaign prospect: 30 points
- Years since last gift
  - Lowest through 2: 10 points
  - 2.01 through 5: 5 points
  - 5.01 through 10: 2 points

Arts: Single-Point System

- Attendee: 1 point
- Subscriber: 1 point
- Arts background: 1 point
- Other arts giving: 1 point
- Donor: 1 point
- Gave in last five years: 1 point
- Gave five or more gifts: 1 point
- Managed/assigned: 1 point
- Researched: 1 point
- Visited: 1 point
- Attended an event: 1 point
- Trustee: 1 point

Arts: Weighted System

- Attendee: 5 points
- Subscriber: 20 points
- Donor: 5 points
- Gift count:
  - 10 or more gifts: 10 points
  - 5 to 9 gifts: 5 points
- Manager: 20 points
- Any board or group membership: 5 points per board/group
- Total contacts × 3 = points
- Current campaign prospect: 30 points
- Years since last gift
  - Lowest through 2: 10 points
  - 2.01 through 5: 5 points
  - 5.01 through 10: 2 points
- Arts background: 5 points
- Other arts giving: 5 points

After producing a score for all records, compare the previous seven years of giving to the capacity by different cut values of the connection score. This will provide a risk adjustment according to various levels of connection. Even determining a single point in the scoring model where a person might be considered connected will enable you to more effectively clean the portfolios. This way, not only are you comparing managed prospects versus the apex of the database, but you can also compare managed prospects to the *connected* apex of the database.

You may also decide to use a model predicting giving or giving at the major level to adjust your projections. In these cases, I will evaluate the capacity versus seven years of giving according to cut values in the model scores. For example, I may have a scoring model of 0–1,000. For the prospects in the 900s, our organization may have closed 15% of their capacity over the last seven years. For the prospects in the 800s, it may be 7.5%. As I project the future close percentages for managed prospects, I may use this model to adjust the outcome. More often, I will use the model to determine the level to ascribe to unmanaged records as I consider portfolio-optimizing scenarios.

INCORPORATING CAMPAIGN FACTORS

I began by stating that the factors influencing campaign feasibility are the funding potential of the constituency, strategy, and execution. With this campaign data, you will be equipped to address all three of these areas.

By evaluating the capacity of the database, identifying the current and projected production, and assessing the risk factors in closing gifts according to connection and management, you will have a good idea about what the database can produce. This is the potential.

In my work, I have seen organizations with one-fourth of another's potential close four times the major gifts. Despite these organizations' lack of capacity, they make up for it in the ability to maximize their existing potential. The way to do this is through strategy and execution.

As you may have noticed, my focus of strategy lies in the major and corporate gifts team. I include planned gifts in this grouping. As you consider your pending campaign, recognize that there are no other areas needing this level of attention. I will discuss annual giving and membership strategies in other chapters. If you are depending on these programs as the primary producers of your campaigns, you are going to have a very hard time. The time for building a major giving program is always *now*. Too many organizations suffer working too hard for too little return.

The strategy I am speaking of is down to the individual major gift prospect level. Each of these prospects warrants the attention of a distinct fundraising department. It is likely you have several prospects that single-handedly could out-give your entire annual fund. Do you pay them the same level of attention? Have you identified the stars you need to align for these prospects to realize their philanthropic potential with *your* organization?

From an analytics perspective, capacities, targets, dates, and asks alone can indicate whether gift officers are truly working prospects. Often, I am asked, "If you were to build a prospect management and tracking program, where would you start?" My answer is always the target. I want to know how much we are asking for and when. This shows me that we have a strategy. All other codes revolve around this code. I can determine the effectiveness of the strategies by evaluating the target efficiency. If for some reason the target remains consistently lower than the capacity rating, we have an issue with cultivation strategy or research. It is hard to defend a discounted target when a gift officer has an entire campaign to work the strategy. If there is no chance of warming a relationship in five to seven years, should the prospect even be in the portfolio?

Most major giving managers start by evaluating execution. Execution without a strategy is risky business. However, with a solid strategy in place, it is the easiest of the three factors to measure. Some metrics for evaluating execution include:

- Number of contacts
- Number of personal visits
- Number of discovery calls
- Target accuracy
- Close yields
- Dollar goals
- Days in stages
- Number of visits per closed gift
- Time from discovery contact to close

Occasionally, these metrics will oppose each other when used as performance goals. At a few client institutions, I noticed major gift officers will have contact goals without having dollar goals. Common contact goals might be 15 visits per month or 20 visits per month, with 5 of them being discovery visits. When preparing for a campaign, it is difficult to optimize the portfolios by capacity because the major gift officers know their portfolio. It is easier to achieve the visit metrics by seeing people they know.

If they were encouraged to take on higher-level, new prospects without having an increased dollar goal, there is no personal incentive to make a shift.

Some client institutions have annual dollar goals, but do not provide an incentive for going above the goal. Frequently, at these institutions, you will see declining numbers in the fourth quarter. The gift officers may have met their annual goals already. If there is no incentive to exceed the goal, they will wait to close gifts until the next fiscal year.

Even if these metrics are not used as goals, they are excellent gauges of performance when applied uniformly to the team, and they enable you to assess the targeting data to determine realistic projections for the campaign.

Case Study

The following outline summarizes the methodology I used at one institution to plan for a campaign and incorporate analytics into the process.

I. Planning
   A. What are the key questions as we plan for this campaign?
      1. *Potential:* Do we have the prospects and capacity?
      2. *Strategy:* Can we appropriately prioritize and target to achieve our goals?
      3. *Execution:* Can we execute our strategies and achieve the necessary production?
   B. How will we answer these key questions?
      1. *Potential:* Calculate capacity of database and prospects.
      2. *Strategy:* Evaluate portfolios, target metrics, and suspect qualification.
      3. *Execution:* Determine existing production and project future yields.
   C. Calculate a gift-based projection as a baseline.
      1. Identify steady production (annual giving).
      2. Project steady production using a linear model.
      3. Identify volatile production.
      4. Project volatile production using the best fit for the trend line (polynomial, logarithmic, etc.).

D. Compare the capacity of closed deals from the volatile trend line to deployment levels and yield during that time period.

E. Apply the same rates to overall capacity to determine potential and required ramp-up metrics.

F. Consider the top of the pyramid. Campaigns will succeed or fail on the back of 1% of your constituents. This apex of your pyramid is the most important factor in fundraising.
   1. Do you know the wealthiest individuals in your pyramid?
   2. What is the capacity of the very top? This group requires the full attention of research.

G. Evaluate the business processes of campaign fundraising:
   1. *Prospecting/pool development:* How does our organization go about building our lists? What is missing or needed to conduct this campaign?
   2. *Pipeline management:* Do we have a process in place for feeding and managing the overall pipeline?
   3. *Prospect relationship management:* Do we have a process in place for managing the specific individuals and corporations on our pipeline?
   4. *Broadbased communications:* Is our process of feeding the pipeline and engaging constituents in place to realize our steady sources of production (mail, phone, online, events, etc.)?

H. Are we adequately staffed?
   1. Measure the cost-benefit ratios of gift officers.
   2. Measure the output of operations staff and analysts (understanding the pipeline in the early stages too).
   3. Are we under-investing in staff?
   4. What is the measured opportunity risk?
   5. Can optimized processes (e.g., macro-level prospecting, technology investments) increase output?

I. Determine your officer performance metrics:
   1. How does staff provide value to your organization?
   2. Are there elements that can be measured?
   3. Which data have an impact on results, rather than untested assumptions and rules of thumb?

J. Determine your program performance metrics.
1. What makes your campaign successful?
2. Which metrics indicate your growth and success?
3. What will it take for us to measure and report on these elements?
4. Can we score our institutional performance?

II. Incorporating Analytics into the Campaign Planning Process
A. Build a comprehensive capacity score:
1. Consolidate past screening data, internal capacity ratings, targeting information, previous giving, and appended census data.
2. Apply a formula to all records to produce one score.
B. Evaluate capacity information, giving trends, and prospect management information.
C. Project future performance from a data perspective.
D. Results:
1. *Capacity:* The ultimate amount a person could give in an ideal scenario over five years.
   a. The average capacity of managed prospects is $425,235.
   b. Unmanaged individuals average $14,015.
2. *Managed Giving*
   a. The average managed prospect gave $41,500 in the previous five years.
   b. Giving yields for managed prospects.
   c. In the past five years, managed prospects gave approximately 5.9% of their capacity.
3. *Yields, Giving, and Capacity by Manager*
   a. *Targeting:* Very few managers are recording target ask amounts (77 total in system). The median is targeting 46% of previously known capacity data.
4. *Researched Suspects and Prospects Scenario:* Managed versus unmanaged
   a. Projected yield with current prospect base. If the following performance is retained:
      i. Maintain the observed yield of 6% for managed prospects.
      ii. Yield 0.6% for unmanaged constituents.

        iii. Keep an existing 2,200 constituents under management.
     b. Then the projected yield would be:
        i. It is likely that the amount raised from this base, with these practices, in five years, will be approximately $70 million.
  5. Optimized Yield Scenario:
     a. Reallocate portfolios to the top 2,200 prospects in the system by capacity (rather than existing assignments), and maintain the same yield percentages.
     b. It is likely the amount raised will approximately double to $135 million.
  6. Optimized Plus Performance Yield Scenario:
     a. Reallocate portfolios to the top 2,200 prospects in the system by capacity (rather than existing assignments), and increase the managed prospects' yield to 10% of portfolio capacity.
     b. It is likely the amount raised will be approximately $225 million.
  7. Industry Standard Yields with Database Potential Scenario (industry standards are three to four prospects per gift at capacity levels)
     a. Use the combined database capacity with these metrics: 25–33% yields
     b. The potential for closed gifts is between $500 and $700 million over five years.
III. Findings
  A. Potential (prospects)
  Strong potential, with a healthy *prospect base* and effective *research*. (Unmanaged yet researched prospects exceeded the capacity and count of existing managed prospects)
  B. Strategy (prioritization and targeting)
  Challenges in strategic development, with many high-level prospects *not managed* and *targeting* data not in place.
  C. Execution (production yields)
  Opportunities for *increasing production* to higher levels and even industry standards.

CAMPAIGN PYRAMID

The most common campaign planning tool is the campaign pyramid. This spreadsheet or series of spreadsheets lists the gifts needed by level, the prospects needed to achieve the gifts, and the suspects needed to qualify the prospects. Several formulas exist for the gifts needed by level. Most include a lead gift at approximately 10% of the overall goal. As campaign totals grow through the roof, the 10% lead gift is less common. More often, the numerous initiatives of the campaign have separate pyramids rolling up into an overall total. The following table shows a simple example of a campaign pyramid.

Gift Level	Gifts	Total Dollars	Prospects	Suspects
$5,000,000	1	$5,000,000	3	9
$1,000,000	6	$6,000,000	18	54
$500,000	12	$6,000,000	36	108
$250,000	20	$5,000,000	60	180
$100,000	65	$6,500,000	195	585
$50,000	100	$5,000,000	300	900
$25,000	250	$6,250,000	750	2,250
$10,000	450	$4,500,000	1,350	4,050
<$10,000	Many	$5,750,000	NA	NA
Total	**904 Major**	**$50,000,000**	**2,712**	**8,136**

As you can see, this pyramid shows a 10% lead gift of $5 million. It also follows industry rules of thumb that it takes three prospects to get one gift. And it follows industry standards that it takes three suspects to get one prospect. I describe the definitions of suspects and prospects in Chapter 5. From suspect to gift, this reflects an 11% close ratio.

When I build a campaign pyramid, I prefer to wait until after I conduct some analysis of the database capacity and the current close metrics. If you historically close 6% of the capacity of suspects and prospects, the industry standard is too aggressive to be an effective planning document. Often times, the close ratios at different gift levels vary considerably. I used the actual close metrics by level to design the pyramid. The following table shows a pyramid adjusted to reflect actual close metrics.

Gift Level	Gifts	Total Dollars	Prospects	Suspects	Close %
$5,000,000	1	$5,000,000	5	18	5.6%
$1,000,000	6	$6,000,000	22	75	8.0%
$500,000	12	$6,000,000	43	110	10.9%
$250,000	20	$5,000,000	77	255	7.8%
$100,000	65	$6,500,000	225	657	9.9%
$50,000	100	$5,000,000	325	945	10.6%
$25,000	250	$6,250,000	765	2,125	11.8%
$10,000	450	$4,500,000	1,422	2,670	16.9%
<$10,000	Many	$5,750,000	NA	NA	NA
Total	**904 Major**	**$50,000,000**	**2,884**	**6,855**	**Ave: 10.2%**

Frequently, I also split the close likelihoods into separate categories for connected constituents and unconnected constituents. I will use either a simple ranking system or a predictive model and calculate the ratios by capacity level layered within connection level.

After you have completed your final planning pyramid, you can fill in the prospects qualified, prospects needed, suspects identified, and suspects needed to inform your campaign prospecting plan. The following table is a sample of the same pyramid with the prospecting information included.

Gift Level	Based on Target Ask Amounts			Based on Capacity Rating		
	Prospects	Qualified	Needed	Suspects	Identified	Needed
$5,000,000	5	2	3	18	12	6
$1,000,000	22	11	11	75	34	41
$500,000	43	12	31	110	45	65
$250,000	77	34	43	255	134	121
$100,000	225	112	113	657	334	323
$50,000	325	124	201	945	454	491
$25,000	765	433	332	2,125	765	1,360
$10,000	1,422	467	955	2,670	1,256	1,414
Total	**2,884**	**1,195**	**1,689**	**6,855**	**3,034**	**3,821**

FINAL THOUGHTS ON CAMPAIGN ANALYTICS

Campaign totals continue to rise as competitive pressure increases. Boards are requiring more from their fundraising executives. Executives are expecting more from their staff. When goals seem unachievable, or your program is stretched, always start with the facts. Leading with numbers is the best strategy for tackling difficult situations.

The data points I emphasized were constituency potential, strategies in place to tap that potential, and the ability and scale of your staff to execute the strategies. By aligning your metrics to these areas, it will be possible to bring your board specific areas of investment to achieve these goals. And if the goals are not feasible without investment, you have arrived at that conclusion after careful consideration.

It is healthy to continually stretch your goals, and it is appropriate to increase the investment in fundraising to reach these goals. It certainly does take money to raise money. Funding your priorities and providing your important services to your communities far exceed keeping the cost to raise a dollar low. At the same time, being a good steward of the money entrusted to fundraising will increase confidence that the money is well spent. By incorporating analytics into your campaign planning, you will be equipped to better steward organizational investment and reach your ultimate goals.

CHAPTER 5

Data-Driven Prospect Management

My line of work enables me to see a great variety of fundraising organizations in various stages of campaign fundraising. Some organizations struggle with unachievable goals, while others in similar circumstances seem to close gifts with ease. A common question I field is "Why are they so successful?" Or, more frequently, I hear, "How come we are not that successful?"

As I explore the management of for-profit industries, I see the same types of questions. We look to the industry leaders for answers. I have seen literature promoting open environments to boost employee morale. I have also seen a focus on dedication and concentration, with clear definitions of roles. Common to nearly all the literature is a focus on the customer. Many of the recent shifts in business focus on managing the relationship with the customer. Through systems of mass customization, targeted individual service, and information gathering, companies are focusing on customer relationship management.

The most successful fundraising institutions have solid prospect management programs. Organizations that seemingly out-raise their potential have dedicated systems focused on their constituents. The entire organization revolves around the prospect relationship.

In the past 10 to 15 years, the majority of major gift fundraising programs have converted from transactional database systems to prospect relationship databases. The previous databases existed solely to make sure that gifts would reconcile. The new databases can still manage the gift accounting, but their focus is much broader. These systems manage many more dimensions of the prospect, including address history, interests, activities, relationships, engagement strategies, and ratings. The database has evolved from a digitized file cabinet to a relevant player in the fundraising organization. It is the brains of the organization and the close friend of the analyst.

Certainly, database systems have their limitations. Bobbie Strand, an industry trailblazer in the prospecting world, will often remind me that having a system that tracks prospect management does not mean you have prospect management. Nonetheless, equipping your database to track these metrics will enable your leadership to manage the program and your gift officers to manage their portfolios.

What does it mean to have systemized processes focused on your constituents? What are those elements common to the leaders in the fundraising world?

ELEMENTS OF SUCCESSFUL FUNDRAISING ORGANIZATIONS

The common elements for successful fundraising organizations are:

- Nature of the constituency
- Identification and prioritization of the prospect pool
- Integration into a prospect pipeline
- A major gift mentality
- A culture of solicitation-focused case stating

Nature of the Constituency

Each organization maintains its own unique collection of the individuals and organizations connected to it through programs, services, or giving. This list is among the most valuable asset any organization owns. No other organization has your list of names, and many would pay to get your list. No other organization has the information you maintain on those individuals closest to you.

At the same time, the grass is always greener in an aspirant peer's database. As a fan of the Minnesota Twins, I often dreamed that we might spend the same kind of money as the New York Yankees. If we only had their line-up, we would be winning series left and right. But, despite the very different salary situations, the Twins manage to be a relevant team most years. They realized they needed to focus on strengths and play fundamental baseball. They could not count on clutch homeruns. Instead, they would have to lay down a bunt here and there and forward the batters.

Your constituency is the least changeable of the elements. Certainly, some organizations benefit from having a wealthy constituency. In many prominent universities, the loyalty is so engrained before a student even graduates that the work seems easy. It is important to note that "who they are" rarely changes—but you can affect "how they think about you."

Identification and Prioritization of the Prospect Pool

Much of the focus of this book is on the identification and prioritization of the prospect pool. You may have little control over who your constituents are, but you have tremendous control over how to spend your time and resources. Devoting individual attention to the people and companies with the highest ability and likelihood to give to your organization is so important that leading fundraising organizations have prospect research departments of a larger size than similar-sized organizations' entire major gifts team. They realize that a handful of people can double a campaign size in some cases.

Concentrating on the top of your pyramid is good stewardship of your resources. Giving the same attention to all constituents regardless of ability appeals to our conscious sense. However, we are paid by the same nonprofit dollars that benefit our constituents. Using this money to maximize potential revenues is the best way to treat all of our constituents fairly.

Integration into a Prospect Pipeline

In Chapter 4, I highlighted the three primary pillars of campaign feasibility: potential, strategy, and execution. Identifying and prioritizing the prospect pool is only discovering the potential energy of your organization. To turn this potential energy into kinetic energy, you need to execute the right strategies to advance the relationship with prospects into major philanthropic expressions. The pool of prospects is only as good as the pipeline that advances the relationship.

I have seen many organizations invest tremendous resources in prospecting. They will hire trained researchers to build wonderful profiles on top prospects. They will build a team of prospect identification specialists devoted to quick qualification of new names for the major giving team. They will have dedicated data mining professionals prequalifying pools for the prospect identification specialists. And they will have beautiful prospect information screens on their database. Yet the new leads just sit there, going nowhere. Why mine for precious minerals if you are going to leave them piled up at the entrance to the mine?

The best organizations have a documented and implemented system for moving identified prospects from the first indication of potential through stewardship of their major gift.

A Major Gift Mentality

In the fashion industry, you will often hear that style is every bit how you wear the clothes. There is an attitude in how you carry yourself. Models can get away with outlandish outfits if they can "sell it" with their attitude.

Some high school football teams have long histories of winning records. High schools of the same size will have the same random odds of getting talented players for their teams. How do some consistently win? You will hear people say "They must put something in the water!" These teams have a confidence in their abilities. They expect to win. The attitude and belief wins the mental contest over the other team.

Long-distance runners are often said to be competing against themselves. It is a sport of heart and determination. Many times, runners will defeat other racers with seemingly superior physical conditioning because of personal drive.

Some nonprofits have a seemingly easy time bringing in major gifts. They have such a natural confidence in the importance of their mission and the loyalty of their constituents that they may even expect to get major gifts. They envision themselves as the type of charity major philanthropists would want to support. They wear this confidence in visits with prospects. They communicate this pride to their constituents. And the feeling is contagious among new staff and volunteers.

At the same time, I have been to many organizations with the complete opposite of this confidence. They do not think of themselves as the recipients of major gifts. You will hear phrases such as, "We are third, after the donors' churches and alma maters." They do not ask for what their services warrant. They ask for what they think they can get. I see this especially in arts and cultural organizations. But many health care, education, and religious organizations carry themselves in this manner. The lack of self-confidence is contagious among new staff, and it becomes difficult to enlist volunteers.

Organizations with the assurance to ask their board members to step up and give true major gifts have what I call a major gift mentality. They do not under-ask. And they raise a lot of money.

Culture of Solicitation-Focused Case Stating

Having a clear understanding of the case for support and using this understanding to move prospects to solicitation without needless delay is a sign of a healthy major gifts program. Earlier I described the concept of the value portfolio. When a gift officer or volunteer clearly understands the purpose of the organization and its case for support, it is easier to listen to prospects as they reveal shared values. Aligning these values is primary for moving to solicitation in a short amount of time.

Some gift officers will hear industry standards that say it takes five to six visits to close a major gift. Accordingly, they will plan on taking this much time with each of their prospects. Obviously, all prospects warrant their own cultivation strategy. Some invested constituents do not need multiple visits to make their gifts. At the same time, some deferred gift options may require numerous visits to coordinate all of the details. It is better to move appropriately without delay unless it is warranted. For most gift officers, delays come from the gift officer's lack of planning, not from the prospect.

PROSPECT MANAGEMENT

Of all of these common elements for leading institutions, the only one where your control is limited is your constituency. You cannot control who they are. But, if you identify those closest to you, engage them with appropriate strategies, maintain a confidence in your institution's worthiness, and maintain a dedicated focus on case-stating, you will see a potential in your constituents that may surprise you.

The coordination of these elements across your organization and with your constituents is what is called prospect management. It is finding clarity in your business processes and integrating all of your efforts for a common goal.

When I build prospect management programs for organizations, I use the following ten steps:

Step 1. Map Out the Big Picture.
Map the business process, from the anonymous name in the database to the major gift donor in stewardship.

Step 2. Develop the Coding Structure.
Determine which elements should be tracked on your database and how.

Step 3. Define the Roles.
Determine who is responsible for entering the data, managing progress, and building and distributing reports.

Step 4. Document the Procedures.
Document the process and the coding structure from identification through stewardship.

Step 5. Train.
Train the organization as a group and individually on responsibilities.

Step 6. Build your Reports.
Write reports for organization progress, for managing staff, and for managing prospects relationships.

Step 7. Develop Assignment Strategy.
Define your process for moving prospects through the process between departments and managers.

Step 8. Develop Prospect Management Meeting Strategies.
Set a schedule and agenda for regular action-oriented discussion of prospect movement.

Step 9. Allow a Ramp-Up Period.
Set aside a period of time to become acquainted with the process and responsibilities.

Step 10. Metrics.
Develop and implement methods of measuring and stimulating individual and organizational performance.

I purposefully leave metrics for the end of the work plan. It is a fruitless effort to institute metrics when you have no shared understanding of the purpose of the system. For staff to be measured, they need to believe that participating in the activity set out in the prospect management plan will benefit both themselves personally and the organization. They will need to have confidence that the system will work. And they need to see the organizational commitment to the process from the very top of the organizational chart.

Map Out the Big Picture

Map the business process from the anonymous name in the database to the major gift donor in stewardship. Earlier, I suggested that development has three primary elements defining the business process. These are base development, prospecting, and major giving. To map out the business process of major gift fundraising for your institution, you should start with these broader areas in mind. Let's review the prospecting and development diagram (Exhibit 5.1).

This approach depicts a funnel and a cycle. The funnel represents the prospecting process, and the cycle represents the work of your major gifts and donor relations teams. Your annual giving and membership programs broaden the top of the funnel to feed more names into the process. Your prospect management systems should start by tracking the progression through this process, from prospecting through stewardship.

Throughout this progression, there are ways we describe individuals or corporations, and there are ways we describe the work we are doing. You will hear words like "prospect" or "suspect." These describe what an individual or corporation *are*. You will also hear words like "qualify" or "solicit." These are words that describe what we *do* to advance a person through the process.

Anonymous Records   If we imagine this process to be chronological over the life of the donor, we need to start before we know the person. The majority of your database will not be known to you. These are the anonymous records. Annual giving and membership programs exist to manage the anonymous records. Through their work, they engage the anonymous donor and bring them closer to the institution. They build up a data picture initially by gathering transactional and contact information.

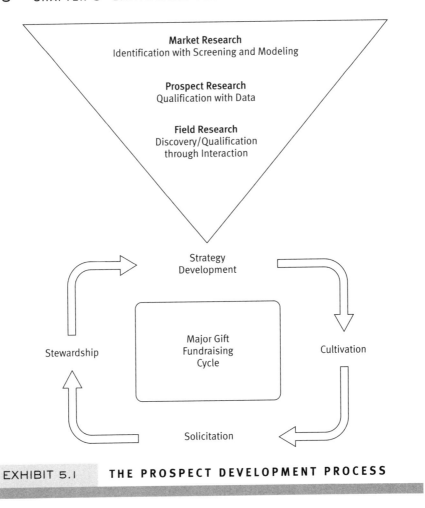

EXHIBIT 5.1   THE PROSPECT DEVELOPMENT PROCESS

For many organizations, the relationship begins long before individuals are anonymous records in our fundraising database. In health care, receiving care may start the relationship. In education, the relationship starts when they receive the first admissions packet as a prospective student. For this exercise, I am starting with their entry into our database.

Suspects   At some point in the process, we discover that an individual or corporation may have the ability or inclination to give a major gift through outright or deferred means. This indication may come from many sources. There are sources that happen more naturally, such as referrals from other donors or volunteers, stories in the news, sudden spikes in annual giving, and so on. And there are sources that describe work we did to identify this potential. These sources are data mining, wealth screening, systematic peer review, and surveys.

At this point, we have little *proof* of the individual's or corporation's actual likelihood to make a major gift to us. However, we have a good *indication* of this possibility. Up until this point, a gift officer has not met the possible major donor. The prospect researcher has not collected any data specifically for this individual or corporation to verify this possibility. The potential gift remains just that—potential.

These are the records in the database that are frequently called *suspects*. In some organizations, they are called *leads*. The terminology in this case is not important, as long as the understanding is shared throughout your organization.

Suspects are measured primarily by the capacity metric. They are often prioritized using predictive models and other indicators of inclination. Once a suspect is identified, the capacity and inclination are generally verified through individual-level data gathering. This work is called research qualification.

Research Qualification   The next step of the process is to gather data at the individual level to support or disprove the indication that an individual or corporation is a suspect. As discussed in Chapter 3, this work uses the same sources of traditional prospect research. It looks into the public assets and income information found in public company filings, private company reports, real estate assessments, foundation records, news stories, and other sources. However, the work is less exhaustive than creating full research profiles.

Many organizations have dedicated prospect identification specialists to conduct research qualification. Since it does not make sense to spend too much time on names that might not enter the pipeline beyond this point, it is necessary to be efficient in research qualification. These specialists need to make quick choices based on limited findings. I generally view 60 to 90 minutes as the maximum amount of time to spend. Some researchers are more comfortable using indicators and flags to make ballpark estimates. Some researchers are more comfortable gathering all the facts and conducting a detailed analysis. The former group is a better fit for research qualification.

Qualified Suspects   After research qualification, a suspect either re-enters the base development pools for annual giving solicitations or moves forward through the prospecting process. If, as a result of the research qualification, the status as a suspect is verified, I like to give the individuals or corporations a unique code to separate them from unqualified suspects. I call them qualified suspects.

Qualified suspects are not yet prospects, because the major giving staff has not yet met them in person. However, they present a greater probability of entering the major giving cycle than unqualified suspects. When I feed the discovery process, I always focus on allocating qualified suspects first, unless our research team does not have the scale to feed the major gifts team. Over time, you can measure the cost benefit of prequalifying suspects versus seeing unqualified suspects. If the success rate of deploying gift officers to unqualified suspects is comparable to the success rate of seeing qualified suspects, or if the cost of the research does not cover the difference in efficiency, it may not be necessary at your institution. I have not seen this to be the case for high-level suspects. However, at a mid-range of giving capacity, this might make sense for your institution.

Discovery   After suspects are qualified with data, they are allocated to the major gifts team or the leadership annual giving team for field qualification. These managers will make contact with the qualified suspects to verify the suspects' capacity and propensity through the field visit. These visits are purposeful and must end with the answer to the question, "Is this a prospect?'

The possible answers to this question are "yes," "no," and "not yet." If the answer is "yes," they must enter the major gift development cycle. If the answers are "no" or "not yet," they will typically re-enter the base development process to either sustain their existing giving or increase the engagement to prepare for future cultivation possibilities.

When I sketch out a business process, I always make a big note where management of the process changes hands. In most business processes, these areas present the biggest clogs in the pipeline. In fundraising, the most prevalent clog is the hand-off of names from the prospect research office to the major gifts team for field qualification.

Up until this point, the research team knows the most about these individuals. Through their qualification work, they have made the case to themselves that these suspects warrant cultivation. To the major gift officer, this is often the first time seeing the names. It is important for the researcher to break it down to the individual level for the gift officer. Researchers should discuss one name at a time and explain why they should go see *this person*. It is important to remember that major gift officers are specialists at one-to-one communications. They are not list managers. Researchers take lists and convert them to one-to-one projects. Do not provide a list to major gift officers. Anecdotally, I have observed this difference. If you have five names to forward to a gift officer, it is better to give them five sheets of paper. If you gave them one sheet listing all five, they might call on one of them. If you separate them, they are separate projects to be worked independently. They might call all five.

I have used the analogy of the ramp meter. In busy metropolitan areas, entrance ramps to freeways are metered with stoplights permitting one car every time it flashes green. By pacing out the merging traffic, the meters prevent clogging traffic with a sudden glut of vehicles. As part of your prospect management system, you should always be mindful of clogging the system with too many new qualified suspects.

Prospects   Only after an individual or corporation is qualified as having the capacity and potential to make a major gift by outright or deferred means do I qualify that entity as a prospect. The word "prospect" has varying definitions across the industry. However, the most common definition is an individual or a corporation under individual management with the qualified capacity and propensity or interests to make a gift at the major level. After the discovery call, it is important to assign all prospects for management.

For suspects, the primary measurement used to determine level and prioritization is the capacity rating. For prospects, the primary metric is no longer the capacity rating—it shifts to the target ask amount. Campaign pyramids that list the prospects by level according to their capacity level are inadequate. Prospects should be listed by their ask amounts. If a prospect is able to give $1 million but will be asked for $100K, that prospect should not be on the $1 million line of your pyramid.

Up until this point, we have alternated between what constituents *are* and what *we do*. Once a constituent is classified as a prospect, it is unlikely they will change in classification. Even after they give a major gift, rarely do organizations change their thinking from prospect to donor. Largely, this is because the best prospects are previous donors. However, what we do changes significantly for prospects.

Cultivation Strategy   The first thing every gift officer should do with a new prospect is to write out the cultivation strategy. As technologically minded as I am, I still recommend pen and paper. It is important to capture the key elements from research and the discovery call to plan this strategy. Below are the questions to ask yourself:

1. Is the capacity rating reasonable? If not, discuss your reasons with the Prospect Research Department to help refine the rating.
2. How much should I target for solicitation?
3. When will I make this ask?
4. What would it take for this prospect to give this level of gift?
   - How can I make him or her aware of our programs fitting their interests?
   - In what ways can I get him or her involved in this program?
   - How can I encourage him or her to eventually take ownership in this program?
   - Who should be involved in this cultivation process?
5. What other information do I need to complete this strategy? Submit this to the Prospect Research department.

Cultivation   The next step in the process is to work the strategy. Cultivating without a strategy is like paying the bills without a budget: You might do it with your own money, but would you do it with someone else's money? Having a cultivation strategy is a responsibility of the gift officer.

You may have realized in the strategy questions I listed the three standard phases of cultivation. These phases are:

- Awareness
- Involvement
- Ownership

Early in the relationship, the activities revolve around building awareness. You may have realized that the prospect's value portfolio aligns with your campaign priorities, but they may not know this yet. They may not know the faculty, doctors, or artists working in the areas of their interests. They may not know there is a peer group of like-minded individuals in your organization.

During the middle portion of the cultivation process, the attention should switch to involvement activities. Now is when you should invite the prospect to join the group of like-minded individuals on an advisory board. His or her participation is essential for developing the third phase of cultivation.

Leading up to solicitation, the cultivation strategy shifts its focus to ownership. The goal is to transition the prospect from participant to owner. If you speak with the highest-level donors to your organization, you will notice they often speak in the first person plural with you about your programs. They might say, "We should focus our energy on student retention," or "We have had such success with our oratorio programming. We should consider outreach into the church community." This is a good sign that the prospect is ready for solicitation.

The specific visits within the cultivation process are traditionally called "moves." Throughout the process, the gift officers should be scheduling these moves and describing them in contact reports. For many researchers, the contact report is the most valuable piece of information to receive from a gift officer. It enables the researcher to follow on leads for more information or other prospects. For the analytics professional, it is a coded sign that a substantive visit took place. For most gift officers, the contact report is the least favorite part of their job. However, with a good cultivation strategy with visit purposes, it can be relatively painless. Below is a sample framework for a contact report:

- Visit details: time, place, etc.
- How did I accomplish the purpose of the visit?
- What new things did I learn about the prospect that might inform or change my strategy?
- How should I change the strategy?
- What do I need to know or do before our next visit?
- When is the next visit?
- What is the purpose of the next visit?

After completing the contact report, put it on the system and notify research if items pertain to them. Some organizations make a point of keeping separate visit strategies from contact reports. I fully support this activity. Having a clear purpose before the visit makes reporting on the visit easier. Additionally, the visits tend to be more productive.

Solicitation   Toward the end of the cultivation process, the gift officer should typically stage the solicitation. Typically, this staging is called the bridge contact. It is a statement of permission to solicit. The bridge may be as simple as, "On our next visit, I would like to present a proposal to you for supporting our campaign initiative." This prepares the donor to receive the proposal and confer with his or her family before the solicitation. At a higher level of solicitation, it is appropriate to present a written proposal.

In prospect management, there are many behind-the-scenes elements of the solicitation process. The gift officers will seek detailed financial advice from prospect research. They must write the proposal. Then they must track how much will be asked, for what project, and when. After solicitation, they should keep track of the expectations for funding the full amount, a portion of it, or more than what was proposed.

Generally, there is a visit during the cultivation process for closing the gift and coordinating the details. Upon closing the gifts, the gift officer must coordinate with Gift Processing, to make sure the gift is counted according to the Memorandum of Agreement, and with Donor Relations, to plan the stewardship strategy. In most cases, there are three visits in the solicitation stage. These visits are:

1. Bridge or permission to solicit
2. Actual solicitation or presenting the proposal
3. Close

Stewardship   The most predictive variable for major giving is previous major gifts. After a major donor commits to the major gift, a thoughtful stewardship strategy is crucial. I mentioned earlier how major donors view their gifts from an investment part of their brains. Think of your donor relations as your investor relations. Your organization needs to show the donor the impact of their gifts. If you presented a scenario where their values are aligned with your organization's values, good stewardship requires you to show this in action.

A stewardship strategy begins with a target just like a cultivation strategy. However, this is not a monetary target. It is a target date, on which the prospect will re-enter the cultivation strategy stage. The question is, "When should we transition back to cultivation for the next gift?" Typically, in a pledge situation you will plan to wait until the fulfillment of the pledge. In some cases, you may begin sooner than that point.

Practically, stewardship follows three stages:

1. Acknowledgment
2. Recognition
3. Reporting

Immediately upon confirmation of the gift, you need to acknowledge receipt of the gift and thank the donor. Regardless of level, the shortest possible timeline for thanking the donor should be the goal of all advancement services and donor relations professionals.

All donors like to be recognized for their gift in some way. Many prefer private recognition by leadership. Others enjoy the public recognition of their philanthropic accomplishment. As part of the discussions with donors in the solicitation stage, every gift officer should learn how best to recognize their prospect.

Throughout the stewardship phase, the organization should report on the impact of giving to the donors. For very high-level donors, personalized reports showing details from endowment performance to stories from scholarship recipients should be presented in a portfolio. For lower-level donors, mass-produced reports with mass customization letters will suffice.

The Big Picture   As you consider these stages and the circumstances specific to your institutions, sketch out the process as a flow chart. Note who is responsible for each stage and when responsibility changes hands. Exhibit 5.2 is a sample flow chart.

Develop the Coding Structure

Determine which elements should be tracked on your database and how. After you sketch out the business process, it will be necessary that your database track the primary classifications and stages, as well as several other tracking

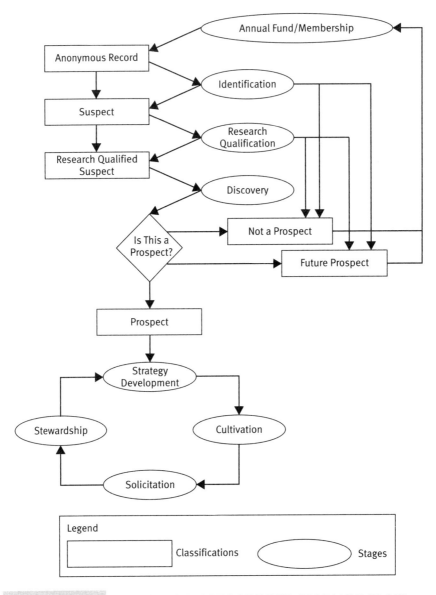

EXHIBIT 5.2   **PROSPECT MANAGEMENT PIPELINE FLOW CHART**

elements. Before you can develop metrics, you need to have the data. The primary elements of your coding structure should be the following:

- Relationship types
- Classifications and stages
- Cultivation strategies
- Proposals
- Contact tracking

Relationship Types   In prospect management, several individuals may manage the relationships with prospects. In all institutions, it is important to capture these relationship types. In complex institutions, it is especially important, as many programs may have a case for seeing the same prospects.

Primary Prospect Manager   The first relationship to code into your system is the primary prospect manager. This is the lead facilitator of the relationship between the organization and the prospect. This individual is not necessarily the one making the solicitation, but he or she holds the responsibility for tracking and maintaining all strategy information and progress towards goals. If there are other relationship managers working with the prospect, it is the responsibility of the primary prospect manager to keep everyone informed and in the loop.

When you code a primary prospect manager, it is important that only one officer is coded. But you should also track all of the primary prospect managers historically assigned to the prospect and the dates they were assigned. Also, make sure to code the date the current manager was assigned to the prospect. When you analyze performance, it is better to give credit where credit is due.

Secondary Prospect Managers   Many institutions maintain secondary prospect managers. This is the most common in decentralized universities, where gift officers are assigned based on academic unit. A prospect might be most likely to give a gift to the liberal arts school. At the same time, he may have played collegiate football. There is a good chance he might split his gift with the athletics program. In this case, a liberal arts school manager might be the primary relationship manager, and an athletics gift officer might be the secondary prospect manager.

It is a responsibility of a secondary manager to have a legitimate case for seeing the prospect. He or she must clear all interactions with the primary relationship manager. Although the primary manager does not need to clear his or her interactions with a secondary manager, the secondary manager should never be blindsided. Full communication between managers on cultivation strategies and contacts should be mandatory.

Several institutions code managers specifically for making discovery calls. These managers are called *suspect managers*. This can be a helpful code if you have a program-based assignment and have little indication of the preferred programs of your suspects before you meet them.

Since HIPAA legislation prevented health care fundraising programs from knowing the diagnoses of their suspects, the only way to know a preferred program was to ask the suspect in the discovery visit. Some health care organizations assigned gift officers to specific areas of care or research. For these institutions, they often built program-neutral discovery programs. In these programs, a suspect manager would determine the best fit for the prospect after the discovery call. Then, they would return to the assignment committee with recommendations for assignment.

If you have a suspect manager process at your institution, you should still make an effort in research or through surveys to identify preferred programs of interest. It is very difficult to pass the torch between gift officers. It is better if the suspect manager goes on to become the primary manager.

Leadership Annual Managers   Many organizations are investing in leadership annual giving programs. These programs assign prospect managers to constituents with midrange capacities, future major donors, and qualified suspects. Often their portfolios are much larger than major gift officer portfolios, because they visit more people with less frequency. In one visit, they must secure the gift or qualify the prospect for major giving. If you have this type of program, a code like suspect manager or leadership annual manager may be necessary to separate the teams. They will have different metrics for performance, stressing volume more than dollars.

Volunteer Managers   In most high-level cultivation strategies, peer relationships play a valuable role. You should be prepared with a code for volunteer managers. I have fashioned the responsibilities of the volunteer after those of the secondary manager, except without tracking responsibilities.

It is very difficult to ask a volunteer to file strategies or contact reports. However, they are happy to meet with a primary manager to discuss cultivation and contact strategies. Volunteers should be informed and managed, even though they are managers. They should be equipped with appropriate information about the prospects. The primary manager should guide every interaction between the volunteer manager and the prospects.

For the majority of prospects, it will be the primary prospect manager making the solicitation. In some cases, particularly high-level cases, organizational leadership or board members may need to make the actual solicitation. These are called *primary solicitors*. It should still be the responsibility of the primary prospect manager to track and maintain the relationship. They should also get credit for the gifts in your performance analysis. However, as part of the strategy, they are using a different mouthpiece for the solicitation. Generally, the primary manager will set up the solicitation with a bridge statement such as, "On my next visit the President and I would like to present a proposal for your support of the endowment initiative." I often measure the close ratios with primary solicitors versus close ratios of prospects at the same capacity and targets without primary solicitors. Often, the success rate is higher. But this is not always the case.

Classifications and Stages   As I sketched out a sample business process, I discussed several descriptions of what constituents *are*. These are classifications. The descriptions of what *we do* are the stages. Here is a list of the codes.

Classifications
- Suspect
- Qualified suspect
- Prospect
- Not a prospect
- Future prospect

Stages
- Research qualification
- Discovery

- Strategy
- Cultivation
- Solicitation
- Stewardship

An anonymous record on the database does not need to be coded. Certainly, this is redundant. However, the suspect code should be coded. As you develop your campaign pyramids, it will be helpful to have the suspect codes to run simple pivot tables. Both qualified and unqualified suspects make up the broader world of suspects. Most pyramids have one suspect column. I will often use qualified and unqualified suspects as separate columns, depending on the complexity of the institution.

Classification codes can be used for work allocation as well. Prospect identification specialists can always pull a constituent coded as a suspect and proceed to qualify the suspect. After they have completed their work, they would code the suspect a "qualified suspect, not a prospect" or a "future prospect." The future prospects and the disqualified prospects typically continue to get annual fund appeals, but the code remains to prevent duplicating efforts. The specialist will also update the record and add a capacity rating and interests where known.

A gift officer or an assignment committee can always pull qualified suspects for discovery assignment. Upon completion of the discovery work, the gift officer would code the qualified suspect as a "prospect," "not a prospect," or "future prospect." The prospects would move into the cultivation cycle starting with stewardship.

The stages describe the work that is happening. When a suspect is assigned to a prospect identification specialist for qualification, the suspect will enter the *research qualification* stage until the work is complete. When a qualified suspect is assigned to a manager for discovery, the qualified suspect will enter the *discovery* stage until the call takes place. If a prospect is assigned to a major gift officer, they will be in the *strategy* stage until the strategy is complete, and so on.

It is important to have dates associated with the classification and stage fields. Many database systems have this capability. However, some leading systems still do not have this capability. In these cases, you may need to set up an additional date attribute to track the classification and stage changes. Your prospect management system should enable you to track how long constituents remain in classifications and stages. This will vary by gift officer, prospect level, and organization.

Cultivation Strategies Every element of the prospect relationship should be tracked in the database system. For the strategy stage, the key pieces will need to be coded with some free text capabilities for summary strategy information. As you might expect after reading my previous chapters, the target amount is the most important first field to code, along with the target date field and the target projects.

The relationship between interests captured by research and the target project is very similar to the relationship between the capacity rating produced by research and the target ask amount. As identification and qualification efforts search for areas of interest and previous giving, they should classify these interests in a grid aligning with your organizational programs. Upon meeting the suspects in discovery visits and throughout the ongoing process of cultivation, the relationship managers should code which program they plan to target. I might have an interest in international nonprofits, music, and religious topics. But my alma mater might be building a new fine arts building. My manager would need to decide whether it is appropriate to target me for the fine arts building because of my interest in music. Likewise, for the campaign pyramid, my placement as a suspect in the fine arts center planning pyramid would be based on my interest codes and capacity. My placement as a prospect in the fine arts center planning pyramid would be based on my target project and ask amount.

For your cultivation strategy codes, you may wish to use drop-down fields for gift levels. Until a gift officer reaches solicitation, a range might be the best estimate. As you run comparative analytics between targeting data, capacity data, and actual gift amounts, you will need to make choices about where in the range to measure. Will you use the bottom of the range? Will you use the median of the range? Or will you use the average actual solicitation amount for all prospects coded with that target gift level?

I prefer to use actual dollar amounts. I encourage the gift officer to put something down initially and continue to modify it throughout the process. I say, "Imagine you are finished with the cultivation process. Using the information you have right now, what would you put down on that proposal?" After every visit, ask the same question and keep or modify the number.

For the narrative portion of the strategy, it is good to have a free text area for the gift officer to put thoughts down. I have tried to have the gift officers schedule each visit on the actions, tasks, or contacts portion of the database. I have had mixed results doing this and found it not worth the coding effort. However, the thought process is solid. They should sketch out a ballpark plan for each visit in the free text area using the awareness, involvement, and ownership framework, and after each visit, they should modify it if appropriate. In academic circles, I have found curriculum planning to be the most helpful analogy. A teacher might consider what needs to be covered by the end of the semester and block plan the lessons. A gift officer should consider what needs to be covered before solicitation and block plan the moves.

Proposals   When developing the coding structure for coding proposals, you should consider the context of the gift project reports. The primary focus of these reports is:

- What gifts are closing in the next month, quarter, and fiscal year?
- How much should we expect from these gifts?
- Which projects will be funded?

Proposals occur specifically in the solicitation stage. The proposal tracking elements of your prospect management system should track your progress through this stage. The first and most important field is the solicitation amount. This is the actual face value placed on a proposal document or presented verbally to the prospect. This amount should never change after it is coded. The target amount is a working metric that reflects the best estimate at the time. The ask amount is a factual, static metric.

After the gift is solicited, you should maintain a changeable code for the benefit of the officers and your reporting. This amount is an expected amount. Similar to the target, the expected amount is a best estimate at the time. However, this does not estimate what the manager will solicit. Instead, this amount estimates what the manager expects to receive in response to the solicitation. Throughout the closing process, this may increase or decrease.

When the gift is closed, the number is generally recorded by the gift processing department, and this amount is static as well. I find it helpful to maintain a separate code for gifts that are connected to proposals. This amount reflects the portion of a donor's gift that is the direct result of the prospect manager's cultivation and proposal process.

In the proposal tracking section of your prospect management system, you should also track the designations outlined in your proposal. When gift processing enters the gift, they will link it to the appropriate fund. By tracking the designations in your proposal section, you will be able to provide the gift processing professionals with helpful information. Also, you will be able to report specifically what is expected to come in for specific initiatives and subinitiatives.

Some organizations have found it helpful to further track the progress of the proposal, similar to how the stages track the progress of the relationship. This staging is much more specific and generally contains the following types of codes:

- Writing the proposal
- Submitted
- Rewriting the proposal
- Resubmitted
- Negotiating details
- On hold
- Closed unfunded
- Funded

You may see a pending code as well. I have always found this to be redundant with submitted, since both are awaiting a response. If I had to choose the most important codes, they would be *closed unfunded* and *funded*. This coding enables you to track the success rate of the project. Too many organizations have proposals open indefinitely without resolution. If I were to have a code for *on hold,* I would require a recorded task or action for when discussions will resume.

Contact Tracking   As the relationship between manager and constituent develops, it is as important to track individual contacts as it is the broader stages. Each of these contacts should have a date, channel, type, purpose, report, and completion flag.

The date is for practical scheduling purposes. It is also very helpful, as several metrics are based on this code. I recommend, when developing reports, to look at overdue activity. This is simply activity that was scheduled to take place, but did not happen. If this ends up being a performance metric, you should see how changeable the field is. It is an easy code for most officers to "game the system" by simply changing the scheduled date.

The channel simply relates to communication channels: mail, phone, online, in-person, event, and other. I still run across many organizations, even very large fundraising programs, that cannot tell me how many personal visits were made by each gift officer. They do not track the channel of the contacts.

The contact types largely relate to the stages, with some additional characteristics. The purpose of these codes is not to assign stages, but to track the activity within the stages. The types I prefer to use are the following:

- Request research
- Discovery
- Cultivation
- Solicitation
- Stewardship
- Resume discovery
- Resume cultivation

Some databases have research tracking sections. Most do not. Because of this, I like to include a research request code in my contact types so we can apply dates and people to the requests. By having a discovery code, you will be able to pull a distinct report of discovery contacts by gift officer. Likewise, cultivation, solicitation, and stewardship contacts enable you to track how often prospects are visited in each stage and the duration of time between the visits.

The codes *resume discovery* and *resume cultivation* are for future planning. The *resume discovery* code is for constituents coded as future prospects. After the discovery call, the qualified suspect might say, "We should talk in two years after my last child graduates college." Or they might be facing a possible IPO or a promotion and will come into money at a future date. This code will make sure that information does not slip through the cracks. The *resume cultivation* code is a similar placeholder for major donors. As part of your stewardship strategy, you should plan for the date a donor will re-enter the cultivation process. This code makes sure donors do not stay in stewardship indefinitely.

When I set up new prospect management programs, I recommend two free text elements for each contact. These are the *purpose* and the *report*. The purpose is simply a statement or agenda for the contact, written before it takes place. This statement or agenda should flow out of the block plan the gift officer sketched out in the cultivation strategy. The contact report is populated after the contact to describe how the purpose was met, any changes in strategy, the new information learned, and what next steps should be taken.

After a contact takes place, a filled-out contact report field indicates the contact took place. I still prefer to maintain a completed code. As a part of this code, I keep the values *completed* and *closed*. The *completed* field indicates that the contact happened. The *closed* field indicates that the contact did not happen. For overdue activity reports, I exclude closed contacts. The *closed* field allows a gift officer to reschedule a new contact and not have it show as overdue activity.

Define the Roles

Determine who is responsible for entering the data, managing progress, and building and distributing reports. Prospect management roles can be a sensitive subject unless approached with the best interests of the team and the organization in mind. It is important to define the difference between role and responsibility: *Role* describes doing the actual work, while *responsibility* describes being held accountable for the work. In prospect management, there are general department roles and responsibilities as well as individual roles and responsibilities.

In the overall business process, the membership or annual giving program is responsible for developing and engaging the base of support. The prospect development program is responsible for feeding the major giving program. The major giving program is responsible for building relationships with prospects and guiding them to solicitation. The donor relations program is responsible for ushering donors back into the major giving program after they make their gifts. The advancement service program is responsible for maintaining a system that tracks all of these processes and maintains constituent information.

Even though each program has primary responsibilities for part of the process, they also have supporting roles outside of their areas. Major gift officers should continue to secure unrestricted gifts from their prospects for the annual fund. Prospect researchers support cultivation by providing information support and feedback on portfolio composition. Donor relations staffs have many opportunities to refer peers of donors to the prospecting process. Gift processors will often be the first to know of a year-end stock transfer or see a check from a bank requiring high minimum balances.

At the individual level, the manager of the major gift team holds his or her team responsible for meeting their goals. However, they rarely have the skill set to pull the appropriate data to make the important decisions. The major gift officer is responsible for managing the relationship with the prospect. However, the prospect management specialist or researcher will see when activity slips through the cracks and can offer friendly reminders and support.

The primary individual roles in prospect management are:

- Entering data
- Managing progress
- Building and running reports

Entering Data   In a perfect world, every gift officer and fundraising executive will track all activity and information about their prospects. In reality, I have seen more prospect management specialists tear their hair out over this issue than any other. They will say, "How come they don't enter their call reports?" or "I have no idea who they are seeing!"

When people do not enter data into a system, one of the following reasons are usually the case:

- They do not know how.
- They are afraid they might do something wrong.
- Their schedule is overwhelming.

All three of these reasons can be overcome. The first two are usually training issues. The system might be dated and cumbersome. In that case, perhaps the system has outlived its usefulness and a change is in order, or additional staffing to compensate for system deficiencies will be necessary. The last reason may be a simple reality, in which case delegation of activity may be in order. It might also be a failure in time management and/or a lack of willingness to participate in the administrative portion of their job.

The gift officer should be responsible for contact management and the cultivation strategy, at the very least. If your organization is well-staffed with administrative assistants, the role of data entry might pass through these staff members. However, the responsibility for the data remains with the gift officer.

Managing Progress   The primary prospect manager is responsible for the progress of relationships in his or her portfolio. The role of tracking activity as it pertains to this progress might fall to a dedicated prospect management staff member. These professionals are usually part of the prospect development program. The relationship of the prospect management specialist and the gift officer should be a peer-to-peer relationship. One should not hold the other accountable as a support role. Rather, they should be allies in the interest of the relationship. The prospect management specialist should notice when the activity does not match the codes and suggest modification.

Because the major gifts manager will hold the gift officers accountable for their activity and progress on goals, it is important for the prospect management specialists to meet regularly with the gift officers. These meetings should be focused entirely on updating tracking information to reflect activity. I recommend that they go through the entire list of prospects in motion monthly to make sure targets, visits, stages, and classifications are accurate. That way, when the gift officer meets with his or her manager, he or she can have confidence that the reports accurately reflect accomplished work.

Building and Running Reports   During the development of the prospect management system, and often in early phases of the campaign, the advancement services department will construct reports. They will need significant input from major gifts team management, prospect development, and the major gifts officers as they develop these reports. After the reports are developed, the advancement services role should diminish, except for the occasional tweak. Typically, the prospect management specialists run and distribute the reports on an ongoing basis.

A colleague of mine, Jennifer McDonough, shared an approach with me she used for managing reports. I liked her approach and often now recommend the same. She suggested keeping an inventory of reports electronically or even in a three-ring binder. These inventories track each report by name, the purpose of the report, the key data elements, who gets the report, how often, and who is responsible for running the reports. Also in the inventory is a sample of each report for reference.

Name of Report	Purpose	Key Data Elements	Distribution	Frequency	Person/s Responsible
1					
2					
3					
4					
5					
6					
7					
8					
9					
10					

It is a good exercise to go through all the reports at your organization and take an inventory. Most people find out there is great redundancy in the reports. Also, some reports are run every month, even though nobody views them.

Document the Procedures

Document the process and the coding structure from identification through stewardship. If you follow the work plan I have presented, you are well on your way to the documentation of your prospect management and tracking procedures. It is important to capture the entire business process, the coding structure, roles as they align to the steps in the process, reports, and policies in one definitive document. This can serve as a manual for training new staff. Also, it will be of benefit in cases of staff turnover, when seamless service is necessary.

When I document procedures, I aim to serve multiple audiences. First and foremost, I want the comprehensive, unabridged version of the prospect management procedures and policies document. After that, I develop an executive summary and several "cheat sheets" by area. For example, the gift officer sheet will have a basic summary section, a "What do I need to do?" section, and a "How do I do it?" section. For the managers or leadership, I may have only a summary section and relevant reports.

It should be the aim of any organization to document its procedures. However, the majority of organizations I visit only document gift processing procedures, if that. Given that turnover is so prevalent in the fundraising industry, it is risky business to overlook this important step.

Train

Train the organization as a group and individually on responsibilities. After you complete the documentation of procedures, begin producing training materials based on the documentation for both group training and individual training. It is important to have the entire major giving and prospecting team see that they are all hearing the same thing. They will also see that management is not only on board with the process, they are driving it. This will be critical later, when performance is directly connected to tracking elements.

Individual training can be targeted to the level and experience of the person. Some will require many and frequent training sessions. Others may only require a recap of the group content.

The most difficult obstacle to organizational change will be the veterans who feel successful in the current structure. Without their buy-in, it will be tough to convince the newer and less-seasoned staff. I would focus on the benefits and threats of a prospect management system.

Benefits

- Having a systemized prospect management system will enable our organization to manage complex portfolios with simple processes.
- It will help us maintain unified and consistent communication with our constituents.
- Our ability to prioritize and engage major gift prospects as a team will improve.
- The major gifts team overall will have increased ability in keeping on track with cultivation.
- Services and prospecting will be able to better support major gift officer work by anticipating needs at each stage of development.

Threats

- Tracking information in shadow systems, such as spreadsheets and notecards, will present a risk for duplicating efforts, stepping on toes, and sending mixed messages to constituents.
- Individuals keeping cultivation strategies and information in their heads will prevent the ability to benefit from the support of services and will hinder understanding about the factors that lead to successful solicitations.
- Unrecorded histories of prospect relationships do a disservice to constituents at times of staff turnover.
- Lack of participation by key members sends a poor message to new staff.

Build Your Reports

Write reports for organization progress, for managing staff, and for managing prospects relationships. Report writing can begin after the coding structure is set and the roles are defined. However, I like to wait and have the advancement services staff participate in the group training session. When they understand the context for the reports, I find they are more efficient and productive in their design.

There are four primary categories of reports in prospect management:

1. Campaign or organizational progress reports
2. Major gifts management reports

3. Prospect relationship management reports
4. Prospecting reports

Campaign and Organizational Progress Reports   Most fundraising programs maintain adequate reports summarizing gift activity for their program. These reports generally show progress on goals overall, by special initiative, and by source of gift. They also display the status of dollars closed on the gift pyramid, with projections based on quarterly target amounts.

Major Gifts Management Reports   The purpose of these major gifts management reports is for the manager to track the performance of his or her team. They are generally at a summary level, including counts and percentages by officer. It is unlikely that the manager will want to see reports at the individual prospect level, except for very high-level solicitations or immediate pending activity. The most common reports for managing the major gifts team include:

- An overview report of prospects per gift officer by stage
- Prospects per program or initiative prioritized by stage
- A summary report of pending solicitations
- An activity summary measuring pending action, current action, and overdue action
- Suspect discovery progress, including discovery calls made and duration of time since assignment

Prospect Relationship Management Reports   For the benefit of each major gift officer, the services team will need to develop reports specific to the progress of each individual under management. This helps the major gift officers track their progress and manage their portfolios. The most typical tracking reports include:

- Comprehensive portfolio detail reports, including every prospect organized by stage, duration of time in the stage, next contact dates, targeting information, proposal details, and overdue action
- Suspect progress reports with discovery call dates and overdue action

Prospecting Reports   Prospect development programs are often overlooked when it comes to reports. In prospecting and research, there is a need to track progress and manage team activity. Common reports for prospecting include:

- Suspect and prospect portions of campaign pyramids
- Suspect pool reports by project area
- Suspects qualified by month, with activation into portfolios
- Counts of profiles produced
- Records updated by month

Develop Assignment Strategy

Define your process for moving prospects through the process between departments and managers. Previously, I described the way that the most common clogs in a business process take place where responsibility changes hands. The toughest clog for most fundraising programs is the transition from prospecting to major giving for discovery and subsequent prospect management. The reasons for this challenge are several, but they generally fall into one of the following categories:

- Portfolios are already full with names.
- Gift officers do not have confidence in the new names.
- There is no system of assignment.

If portfolios are already full, it is important to determine whether they are full with prospects in active cultivation and whether the managed prospects have higher capacities than the unmanaged constituents. If this is the case, the gift officers have a legitimate reason for shunning new names. If the portfolios are healthy and there is significant unmanaged potential, you must quantify this potential to make the case for investing in more staff. You can do this by calculating the team close ratios for managed prospects, as described in Chapter 4. Then provide scenarios for the unmanaged names by bucketing them in groups of 125 or 150, pulling from the top down by your capacity ratings. Calculate the aggregate capacities of these buckets and determine where the dollars closed by bucket slip below the price point for justifying a gift officer.

There are many reasons to lack confidence in new names provided by prospecting. In some cases, the reasons are legitimate. Perhaps the names being put forward for discovery truly do lack the capacity and indicators of likelihood. Also, the success rate of connecting with these new names might be so low that the manager expects to hit a closed door.

When the constituent relationships are so cold that a manager can't secure an appointment, discovery warming strategies are necessary. These might include targeted discovery events or advance letters. The letters will be along the lines of "In the next couple weeks, we would like to meet with you to discuss our future plans for the campus expansion." This provides an opener for the manager. They can lead a conversation with, "Did you receive the letter?"

The most common cause of poor success in the discovery process is basic contact information. For many managers, if they can't reach the person in the first phone call, they will give up and move on to a person they can reach. Needless to say, finding home and business addresses and phone numbers should be standard in the research qualification process.

Many gift officers have internal filters they use to accept or reject names provided to them by the prospecting department. Often they have different gauges of capacity or likelihood than the research office. I have seen this with private company owners living in modest homes. These are Stanley's "Millionaire Next Door" types. Even though private business owners are among the most philanthropic sector, they do not look glitzy on paper. I also hear managers reject names because the constituent has not given in so long. This might be a chicken-or-the-egg situation. At a certain level, some constituents will not give without the personal attention. Many very wealthy people never open their mail, much less take out the checkbook and send it to the charity. It is not that they are uncharitable. Quite the opposite. Instead, the charity is competing for time with very busy people.

This lack of confidence is precisely why gift officers and prospect researchers should meet often. The gift officer can inform the prospect researcher about why he or she pursues some prospects and not others. If the explanation is reasonable, the prospect researcher can look for the "right" characteristics moving forward. If it is unreasonable, the prospect researcher has an opportunity to provide data to show the value of donors fitting the same characteristics of the qualified suspects referred.

Very few organizations have a solid system of assigning new qualified suspects for discovery. I have seen the most sophisticated prospecting programs build up a pool of great names that just sit there. The same organizations may also have very metrics-based, dedicated cultivation strategies. The hand-off just doesn't work.

An assignment strategy should include the following elements:

- Assignment committee
- Discovery goals
- Dollar goals that support portfolio optimization

The most effective assignment committees have as members the major gifts team manager, the prospect management specialist, the prospecting director, and one or two officers. This group will meet periodically to review the new names and determine who should conduct the discovery work. After discovery, this group reviews the results of the call to determine management for the cultivation process. Most times, the discovery officer will be assigned the prospect for cultivation. However, in suspect manager and leadership annual manager systems, the assignment will change hands.

Common gift officer goals include dollar and activity goals. The most common activity goals are 15 to 20 visits per month. As part of the assignment strategy, and pending the stage of the campaign, these monthly visits should include a number of discovery calls. Early in a campaign, this amount will be higher. Later in the campaign, the focus should shift to closing gifts, and this metric might decrease.

The dollar goals for gift officers should continue to stretch the gift officer. And there should be incentives for exceeding this goal. If the dollar goal is too comfortable, the manager will focus on the activity goals. Activity goals are easier to achieve with stable portfolios. There will be limited willingness to take on new, higher-capacity names where the risk of securing visits diminishes.

If you have a pool of names that continues to collect the proverbial dust, you should discover the cause and then develop and document an assignment strategy that addresses the issues. As your program develops, be willing to continually modify this strategy.

Develop Prospect Management Meeting Strategies

Set a schedule and agenda for regular action-oriented discussion of prospect movement. A data-driven prospect management system also needs traditional methods of communication. Regular meetings to discuss the pipeline, activity, and new potential are necessary and helpful to maintain a healthy system.

I recommend these three meetings take place at least monthly:

1. Team activity meeting
2. Officer activity meeting
3. Officer update meetings

Major gift teams should meet as a group to discuss pending solicitations and cultivation issues. Managers will benefit from each other's advice, and a team approach can develop. It is important for the manager to recognize successes to the whole group. Many gift officers are motivated by competition and recognition of accomplishments.

The major giving team manager should also meet with each officer individually to discuss activity. The focus of this meeting should be progress on goals and performance management. The agendas should be report driven. I would discuss the following:

- Pending solicitations
- Pending action
- Overdue action

The prospect management specialist should meet with each officer individually and before the officer activity meetings. The purpose of this meeting is to update all system information to reflect the actual activity of the officer. This enables a peer discussion of goals before meeting with the major giving team manager. Also, it helps to make sure everything is up-to-date before the reports are produced for the activity meetings.

Allow a Ramp-Up Period

Set aside a period of time to become acquainted with the process and responsibilities. You may have realized throughout this process of developing a data-driven prospect management system that I have had a unique order of steps. I did not start with the metrics and build a system around them. I started with outlining a business process first. Then I presented the components of the process to make sure it works. Metrics should first and foremost help you determine if your processes are working.

When metrics become the subject of prospect management, personal accountability becomes the subject. It is a sensitive subject for most gift officers, and there may be several reasons or excuses why gift officers may not meet their responsibilities. The most common excuses are:

- These requirements do not make sense or have any context.
- The database is not showing what I did.
- I did not know my responsibilities.
- These systems keep changing.
- I did not know how to record this information correctly.

This work plan presents a system for removing all of these obstacles. It starts with the business process to provide context. Then, the system coding is developed to directly fit the context, focusing on reflecting actual activity. The system is documented and used for training new gift officers. This provides assurance that the system will not change, and it provides group and training opportunities with ongoing service from a prospect management peer.

If you cover all of the bases, the only reason a person does not meet goals is actual performance. This provides confidence to the gift officers that the system is immensely fair. If they do the work, the system reflects this. If they do not do the work, the system reflects this. And, it makes the job of managing a team easier for a director of major gifts. If it is not in the system, it did not happen.

As part of the ultimate implementation of this system, you need to realize that it takes time to acclimate the organization. For many, becoming data-driven in prospect management is a great organizational change. If you hold feet to the fire too soon, you will push people away. I recommend a ramp-up period to become familiar with the meeting structures, the system coding, the reports, and the work activity. It may take six months or more to develop any comfort.

A few years ago I studied Kung Fu as a way of getting exercise and broadening my experiences. One phrase I heard several times stuck with me. It takes one hundred repetitions for your mind to learn a move. It takes one thousand repetitions for your muscles to learn the move. The point was that knowing something does not mean you can necessarily do it. You may have all of the elements in place to track and manage prospect development, but it takes time to commit the activities to the organization's muscle memory.

Metrics

Develop and implement methods of measuring and stimulating individual and organizational performance. After a system is in place and working, the next step is to determine the methods for measuring its effectiveness and maximizing its output. When I build any new method of measurement, I follow a process very similar to the beginning stages of the Cross Industry Standard Process for Data Mining. The process again, as shown in Exhibit 5.3, is to develop a clear picture of what you hope to accomplish (business understanding); determine which data elements reflect this business understanding; gather and prepare the data; model; evaluate against the business understanding; and deploy your model.

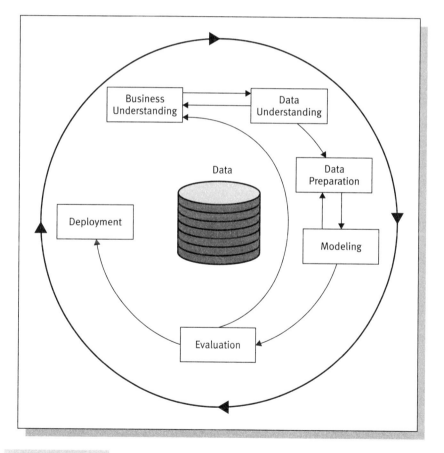

EXHIBIT 5.3   **CROSS INDUSTRY STANDARD PROCESS FOR DATA MINING (CRISP-DM)**

Every project starts by determining the business understanding and then following that with data understanding. If we consider the metrics to be the data understanding, the objectives of our prospect management system constitute the business understanding.

Business Understanding: Objective of Prospect Management   As you set out to determine the objectives of the prospect management system, you should refer back to the original business process. The primary goals of this model are the following:

- *Identification:* Feeding the pipeline with suspects
- *Qualification:* Qualifying the suspects with data and through interaction
- *Cultivation and Solicitation:* Developing strong portfolios, developing cultivation strategies to align case and personal values, "moving" prospects with financial capacity closer to the organization, and soliciting prospects at the appropriate amount
- *Stewardship:* Strategies to "move" prospects back into cultivation

Identification: Feeding the Pipeline with Suspects   How do you determine whether you are successful in identifying new people for major giving? You should consider the volume of names identified and how effectively they work into your system. How efficient is your prospect identification system? Do you have the data to identify prospects? Are you appropriately staffed? Does the staff have the skill sets to identify prospects using diverse methods?

Qualification: Qualifying the Suspects with Data and Interaction   The goal of the prospect identification specialists is to convert lists of identified suspects to individual assignments of research-qualified suspects. How long does it take to qualify a name produced in the identification process? How often are the prospect identification specialists successful in moving individuals and corporations to the next stage of the process? Do you have the staffing and necessary skill sets to accomplish the work you want them to do? Are you appropriately investing in the data sources necessary to do the work? Are research-qualified suspects sitting in a holding tank indefinitely? Are you replenishing portfolios?

Cultivation and Solicitation: Developing Strong Portfolios As you focus on dedicating individual assignments for management, you should consider the cost benefits. Are there ways to maximize a return on investment? Do the portfolios yield their potential? If you modified the composition of the portfolios, would you realize a greater potential? What is the impact of the individual manager on the success of the portfolio? Should you consider realigning prospects and managers to increase your yields?

Cultivation and Solicitation: Develop Cultivation Strategies to Align Case and Personal Values Even highly customized strategies can have commonalities for measuring. You can consider, first of all, whether you have strategies for every prospect in cultivation. Are your gift officers working these strategies? How long does it take to move through the cultivation process? Does this vary by capacity, existing connection, job sector, age, etc.? Should you modify the timeline for future strategies based on average visits per gift among other prospects with similar characteristics?

Cultivation and Solicitation: "Moving" Prospects with Financial Capacity Closer to the Organization Every fundraising executive should ask themselves, "Are we seeing the best prospects?" Is the true apex of your pyramid your first priority? Do you have strategies in place to engage wealthy constituents with cold relationships? What is your success rate at the very top of your pyramid? Does it take more prospects for each top-tier gift than it does for midrange gifts?

Cultivation and Solicitation: Soliciting Prospects at the Appropriate Amount Is your organization among those that lack the confidence to ask a prospect for their capacity? The comparison of giving to capacity is the most telling number for outside counsel to gauge the ability, confidence, and maturity of a fundraising organization. It factors heavily into assessments of feasibility. Are you targeting the capacity of your prospects? Are you soliciting the amounts you are targeting? Are you closing the amounts you are soliciting?

Stewardship: Strategies to "Move" Prospects Back into Cultivation So many fundraising programs focus all of their prospect management efforts on the process of closing gifts. After the gifts are secured, they have no strategies. If the most effective donors are previous donors, effective stewardship processes are imperative. Are your donors thanked in a timely manner? Do donors move back into the cultivation process when they should? Are donors given the same attention as prospects? Should they be?

Data Understanding: Metrics for Prospect Management   After you have a clear understanding of the objectives of each element of the business process, you should consider the data that reflects this business understanding. Your coding systems should enable countless ways to slice and dice each stage. Here are several suggestions of data points for each area.

Identification
- Number of new suspects identified each month or year
- Number and percentage of constituents with wealth information on the database
- Number and percentage of constituents with indicators of propensity
- Frequency of modeling projects
- Number of survey responses on the system
- Presence of a data acquisition plan
- Presence of a data mining and modeling plan
- Cost benefit of screening and data mining projects
- Effect of identification on qualification efficiency (prospect identification specialists reviewing fewer names to find research qualified suspects)

Qualification
- Time it takes to qualify each name; for this data point, you will need to maintain a research log of time spent researching by constituent
- Total suspects qualified
- Number of suspects qualified each month or year
- Number of suspects qualified to produce each research-qualified suspect
- Number of research-qualified suspects with discovery calls made

- Number of research-qualified suspects needed for every successful discovery call
- Total number of discovery calls made
- Discovery calls made per month or year, overall and by manager
- Efficiency of qualification and discovery work relative to capacity level
- Number of capacity ratings on the system
- Percentage of existing portfolios rated for capacity
- Overall volume of the unassigned pool of research-qualified suspects
- Program-specific volume and capacity
- Duration of time between coding a constituent as a suspect and conducting the research qualification
- Duration of time between coding a suspect as a research-qualified suspect and conducting a discovery call, overall and by manager

Cultivation and Solicitation
- Distribution of prospects by geo-demographic profile in manager portfolios
- Distribution of prospects by industry sector in manager portfolios
- Distribution of prospects by capacity and propensity ratings in portfolios (high capacity/high risk, high capacity/low risk, medium capacity/high risk, medium capacity/low risk, etc.)
- Number and percentage of prospects with target ask amounts
- Ratio of target ask amounts to capacity
- Ratio of actual ask amounts to target ask amounts
- Ratio of closed gifts to ask amounts
- Ratio of closed gifts to capacity
- Average capacity of prospects, overall and by manager portfolio
- Average target ask amounts of prospects, overall and by manager portfolio
- Number of prospects by gift pyramid levels, overall and by manager portfolio
- Dollar production, overall and by manager portfolio
- Number of gifts secured, overall and by manager portfolio
- Production by manager within each geo-demographic or industry segment

- Distribution of prospects by stage
- Contact frequency of prospects, overall and by manager portfolio
- Personal visit frequency of prospects, overall and by manager portfolio
- Number of contact reports filed, overall and by manager
- Correlation of contact frequency to gift level, overall and by manager
- Average duration of time between contacts, overall and by manager
- Average duration of time between stage changes, overall and by manager
- Average time from entering strategy to actual ask date, overall and by manager
- Number of prospects with populated cultivation strategies
- Average level of connection or engagement, overall and by manager portfolios (track will increase and decrease over time)

Stewardship
- Number and percentage of prospects with dates to resume cultivation, overall and by manager portfolio
- Number and percentage of strategies in place, overall and by manager portfolio
- Average time to receipt of gifts, overall and by manager portfolio
- Number and percentage of prospects recognized
- Endowment reporting frequency
- Average duration of time from entering stewardship until re-entering cultivation, overall and by manager portfolio
- Average duration of time from pledge fulfillment until re-entering cultivation, overall and by manager portfolio
- Percentage of major donors who give second major gifts

Incorporating the Metrics   After you determine all of the metrics you can use, the next step is to measure the impact of the metrics over time. For this to be possible, you will need to develop dashboard reports and longitudinal tracking models.

The dashboard reports should consist of the key metrics and summaries by area of the business process. A one-page scorecard for each gift officer will enable the major gift team manager to quickly assess each officer. These dashboard scorecards should include the metrics that directly connect to their performance goals first, then include other indicators of progress and performance.

Tracking models are intended to show the growth of populations over time. The most common tracking models are used by alumni relations programs to measure the increase or decrease of engagement levels of the entire alumni body. These same types of models can inform the level of attachment of prospects over time. They will measure whether the work of annual giving or major giving is bringing the pool closer to the institution.

Categories in your tracking model might include:

- How recent the previous gift was
- How frequently they gave
- How much they gave
- Diversity of types and designations of gifts
- Numbers of affiliations
- Participation in a volunteer, board, or advisory capacity
- Event attendance
- Numbers of family or business relationships on the system
- How recently the constituent was contacted
- How frequently the constituent is contacted

After you score all records by the model, you can aggregate the total increase and decrease in attachment by individual, gift officer, all managed prospects, all constituents, or any other subset of the model.

FINAL THOUGHTS

I started my discussion on data-driven prospect management by stating that it was among the greatest of success factors for leading fundraising institutions. I hope the attention I paid to being data driven as you develop or refine your prospect management system gives you some ideas as you better your organizations. Remember, it will take dedication to implement changes in your organization, but they will be worthwhile in the long run.

In the dieting world, the ways to lose weight are relatively simple: Eat fewer calories and burn more calories. If you work hard and stay focused on this process, you will lose weight. However, many people do not succeed, even though they know full well how to lose weight. I count myself among them (off and on in periods of fast-food weakness). Many of the diet programs in the world make a lot of money by advertising quick and painless ways of achieving this goal. They appeal to us because they tell us we can achieve the goal without the work.

In the arena of financial management, get-rich-quick schemes are a dime a dozen, but the same principle is in place. Instead of calories, the topic is money. Earning more and spending less will increase assets. Earning less and spending more will decrease assets. Several experts like Dave Ramsey and Suze Orman teach these basic principles of living within your means, and the principles work. However, you have to work hard to achieve your goals. The supposedly quick and painless schemes seem so much more appealing to our natural sense.

In fundraising, if you make contacts and ask more, you will raise more money. If you raise money without hard work, it is likely you are raising far less than the potential of your database. Think of this outline as the dieting or budget plan that involves doing the right things well and sticking with them. You will raise more money. And your growth will be sustainable.

CHAPTER 6

Annual Giving Analytics

A nnual giving and membership programs were some of the first departments to incorporate analytics into their work. Because many of them are mass mailing and phone programs, they were able to pull strategies from direct marketers doing very similar work. However, of the annual giving and membership programs incorporating analytics, I have found that the majority of them use very generic outsourced models to filter their lists. Most do not build their own models that will predict their own behaviors. Instead, they purchase models showing the behaviors nationally or by industry. The few organizations that have internal predictive modeling capability are able to bring an enormous degree of efficiency into their programs and increase their net production.

To best address the incorporation of analytics into your annual giving and membership programs, I want to start with understanding the business model. In Chapter 5, I described base development as the first primary step of the overall business model of fundraising. If we use the analogy of a pyramid, we see that the larger the base of the pyramid is, the larger the apex will be. If we consider attachment to be a filter for prospecting, what are the processes to build this attachment before we run the model?

Functionally, annual giving programs have two primary roles in the business of fundraising. These roles are:

1. Broadening the base of support by engaging new and existing constituents
2. Building sustained giving relationships to feed the pipeline

As a by-product of these goals, annual giving and membership programs have become the primary source of unrestricted support. For many organizations, these dollars are at such a premium that the dollar goals dwarf the bigger picture. Nonetheless, many directors of base development programs have these goals as a present reality.

To broaden the base means make it larger, or increasing the n. For most organizations, there is a natural constituency. In higher education, there are alumni, athletics attendees, fine arts attendees, faculty, staff, students, and parents. In health care, there are patients, patient families, doctors, staff, and volunteers. In the arts, you have members or subscribers, attendees, resident artists, and staff. In other organizations, the only natural constituencies are existing donors.

The natural constituency is most often the easiest to engage through mass communications. If organizations need to acquire lists outside of their constituency, they will find much lower success rates. As you think about broadening your base, start first by determining whether you have captured the names of all of your naturally occurring constituents. Do you have your athletics database connected to your fundraising database? Do you acquire names at fine arts events or lectures? Perhaps the cost of attending free events is registration. Do you include all of your professionals and staff on your fundraising database?

Perhaps the only thing more important than adding to your base is sustaining the giving relationship. I have always encouraged annual giving directors to put renewal at the top of the list of priorities. It costs so much more to acquire a name than it does to renew a name, and if you do not renew a name within the first year, the likelihood of that individual giving in future years drops considerably. For this reason, about half the organizations I have worked with never ask for an increased gift from first-time donors in the next year.

Although many major donors do not have consistent giving patterns, nearly all planned giving donors and nearly half of major donors do show consistency. In planned giving donors, there is generally much less of an increase in gift levels over the years. With major donors, you will see more dramatic spikes and often space in between these spikes.

Even one major donor can out-give the entire goal of an annual giving program. Annual giving is a very inefficient way of raising money. It is a "high-volume/low-dollar" activity. Major giving is a "high-dollar/low-volume" activity. It will always be a more efficient means of fundraising. However, major giving is nearly impossible without a base of support. Annual giving can exist with or without major giving. However, in pure economic terms, placing annual giving dollar goals above base building to feed the pipeline is completely absurd.

Sometimes, in political terms, the annual giving program's hands are tied. The need for unrestricted support and the failure to acquire these funds by other means will place tremendous pressure on base development programs. I have often said, "The annual fund is a dean's best friend." Deans especially appreciate the unrestricted money to devote to their priorities. A fundraising executive should wear "prospecting-colored glasses" when considering strategies for the base.

I especially see pressure placed on high-volume activities among organizations with immature or no major giving programs. The public broadcasting industry, for example, has a great variety of maturity levels in their programs. Some stations have tremendous sophistication in their major giving efforts, and the membership program feeds these strategies. Others have little to no major giving programs at all. In these programs, the pressure to meet private support goals rests entirely on the membership director. If I had to suggest a "Dirty Job" for the Discovery Channel show, I would offer membership director at a small public broadcasting station. If they don't meet the pledge-drive goals, it could mean the collapse of some of these stations. Out of panic, the membership director will turn to need-based messaging or obligation-based messaging and make things even worse.

I have seen some stations build major giving programs and shift the focus of membership from survival to base engagement. These stations have decided to view themselves as places worthy of receiving major gifts. They have shifted away from "help us" to "let us show you the impact we have in our community." The membership directors are less stressed out, and the stations raise more money—a lot more money.

CONSTITUENT LIFE CYCLES

Consider how for-profit organizations build their customer base. They have rather simple and defined models measuring from entry points or points of first contact through the lifetime value of the customer. But they also consider several areas within this progression. Here are some of those points of consideration:

- Entry points for customers
- Measurements of customer value in terms of transactional recency, frequency, and monetary level

- Up-selling and cross-selling goals
- Public and customer opinion research
- Inventory of all of the touch points where customers interact with their companies
- Geographic distribution—knowing where their customers live and the markets where they do business

Very sophisticated annual giving and membership programs are now considering many of these same goals. Incorporating analytics into your programs will enable you to study these as well.

Entry Points for Constituents

Let's begin by evaluating a sample business model that a for-profit company might use as they consider developing their customers (Exhibit 6.1). They first research and understand the general public to understand which people or businesses fall into their target market. This target market is the individuals or businesses that fit the profile of existing customers or match interests relating to new products or services. From within this target market, they identify the prospective customers. When prospective customers become actual customers, the focus typically shifts to repeating the buying behavior. Once a customer is retained, they will focus on up-selling and cross-selling to increase the customer value. In some cases, very loyal customers will become "rainmakers"—able to feed the organization with more customers through references or referrals.

Now, let's consider this same approach in a higher education institution (Exhibit 6.2). It becomes much more complex because of the entry point. Higher education has multiple entry points. For alumni, the business model must begin before the prospects were even students. For non-alumni, fundraising will often be the original point of entry.

Institutional research studies the general public to identify the target markets for prospective students. In some institutions, they will also research markets in the context of institutional advancement. Admissions or enrollment programs focus on converting prospective students to actual students. The student experience is guided by advisors and faculty. As students graduate and become alumni of the institution, alumni relations will likely be the first voice of a post-academic relationship with the institution. The annual fund may also solicit immediately upon graduation.

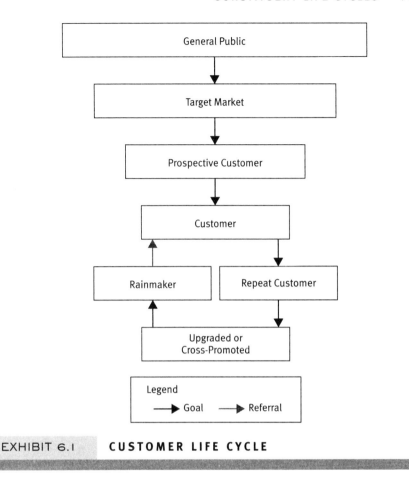

EXHIBIT 6.1   **CUSTOMER LIFE CYCLE**

A common path to donorhood is via alumni association membership. Another path to donorhood, especially for non-alumni, is target market to prospective donor to donor. The target market may be an acquisition list, community members, or referrals. The annual giving program engages the prospective donors. Once the donor is acquired, the next goal is to encourage renewal of this behavior. After the relationship is solidified, the focus shifts to upgrading to major donors. Both major donors and alumni association volunteers may become rainmakers and refer new donors or prospective students to the institution.

Even though this business model seems much more complex, it is a simplification of the entry points. If you consider athletics, fine arts, community services, medical services, speaker events, and all of the other

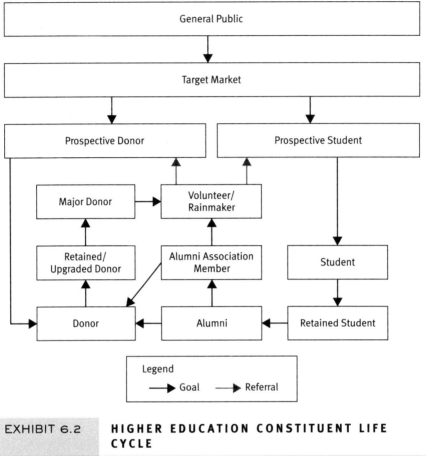

EXHIBIT 6.2   HIGHER EDUCATION CONSTITUENT LIFE CYCLE

services universities and colleges offer to the community, there are many opportunities for constituents to begin relationships.

An unfortunate reality is the specific focus on alumni of the annual fund. A first question I ask of any annual giving director is, "How many of your major donors are alumni?" They should know this if they are feeding the pipeline. In higher education, you may be surprised how few of the major donors actually are alumni constituents. In many public universities, this number is less than half. In cases where the annual giving director is focused on alumni at the expense of engaging all constituents, it is driven more by rankings than the business model of fundraising.

The alumni participation rate is a component of college rankings. Because of this, many institutions have set aside the fundraising business model for the sake of strategies to increase college rankings. An unfortunate by-product of this approach is that many academic fundraising executives lay out alumni participation as the primary metric for the annual giving officer's performance evaluation. What suffers is the overall constituency participation rate. And when participation becomes the sole metric, prospect identification suffers. It mirrors major gift officers' lack of willingness to take new names when their only metric is the visit goal.

Let's use a hypothetical situation to highlight the issue. Let's say an annual giving director was testing two direct mail pieces with random samples. The goal was to identify which piece to send the entire segment for this appeal. The returns came in, and the first piece brought in a 5% response rate. The second piece brought in a 10% response rate. For most directors, the test is complete. They will send the second piece to the entire file. Now let's say we analyzed *who* responded to each piece. What if the returns to the first piece averaged three to four times the giving capacity of the second piece returns? Would you section off the high-capacity individuals and send them the first piece, even if it risks a lower participation rate on the entire mailing?

As you consider the entry point of your constituents, think back to my discussion about giving motivations in Chapter 2. Why do your donors give to you? Maybe it is the following:

- Giving back from a sense of pride in the alma mater
- Impact of the institution on the community or society
- Quality of the academic experience and its impact on life
- Importance of the research for a better future
- To remember or honor faculty or leadership

How many of your constituents learned these things from you? When does someone first develop pride in their alma mater? When does an alumni first witness the impact of their school in the community of society? When do they have their academic experience? When do they learn of the research programs at your school? When are those faculty and leadership relationships made? For the majority of your alumni, their motivations for giving developed long before they received the first letter. Annual giving has the opportunity to tap into these existing feelings so they might be manifested in charitable dollars, and it has an opportunity to connect with the admissions and academic community to consider the entire life cycle of the constituent.

RFM Analysis

One of the most common measures of customer value in corporate America is the RFM calculation. RFM, which stands for recency, frequency, and monetary value, is a fully transactional picture of customer value. It does not consider personal affinities or nonpurchasing activities; rather, it focuses only on purchases made. Specifically, RFM describes how recently a customer made a purchase, how frequently they purchase, and the amount of money spent on a purchase.

Recency   Online merchants are the most conscious of the recency factor. They realize that people make numerous online purchases in single shopping experiences. When they go to a Web site to purchase a CD or book, they are more likely to buy another CD or book during that same visit than to return to make another purchase. Because of this, the merchants will cross-sell heavily within one session. You may see, "If you make $23 more in purchases, you will receive free shipping." Or you may see, "Customers who bought *Fundraising Analytics* also purchased *A Guide to Developing Prospective Donors.*" In addition, they will often send advertisements for additional purchases on the receipts you receive in your e-mail inbox. Department stores such as Target and Wal-Mart effectively tap into the recency metric, too. How often do you go to a department store to purchase one item and end up with a cart full of other products?

Donors who recently gave are the most likely to give next. This might seem like common sense, but you may not have had a name for it. This is why renewal is such a significant source of revenue and among the priorities of your strategies. Even outside of the transactional realm, recency of activity converts well into giving. Patients are more likely to give soon after their patient experience. Athletics donors are more likely to give soon after their team makes a successful run in the playoffs. Alumni will give more after attending a reunion.

Frequency   Another measure of customer value looks at repeat purchasing and transactional loyalty. This measurement is called frequency. You will see the very competitive services industries invest heavily in building frequency. Airline frequent flier programs, hotel rewards programs, and frequent diner cards reward customers for frequenting their establishments.

They realize that the more experiences a customer has with their company, the more often the customer will choose their company over a competitor when a choice is presented to them. It costs more to gain a new customer than it does to renew an existing customer.

Magazine pricing might be the most obvious example of the price difference between acquisition and renewal. The cost of purchasing a single magazine may often be 25% or more of the cost of a 12-issue subscription.

In fundraising, frequency of giving reflects constituent loyalty and increased lifetime value. Typically, frequency analysis will look at both how long a person gives and how consistently they give in this time period. Frequency of giving is among the most predictive variables for giving planned gifts. Because of this, most of the generic models for purchase are built almost entirely by combining consistent giving and age.

Monetary Value   Perhaps the most obvious measure of customer value is how much a customer spends. Even within this metric, there are several views of spending. Companies may look at how much a person has spent over a lifetime and the average amount of each transaction. Or, they may look at the amount of the most recent purchase. Also, they will consider the largest purchase ever made.

For most fundraising organizations, it takes no convincing for them to look at monetary value. The challenge for many places is that monetary value is the only measurement. They may siphon off donors by gift level to major giving without any other criteria. Gift officers may reject a prospect forwarded by metric if the prospect does not already have significant gift history. As important as gift amount can be, without recency and frequency, you will not have the full picture.

Building an RFM Score   There are several ways of combining all of these measurements into one definitive score. The strongest scores will require giving by year for at least 10 or more years, total giving, most recent gift and date, first gift and date, and largest gift. I will often rank the constituents by each of these measures using statistics software and then combine them to produce one overall measurement. I may also use a simple point system to produce a quick snapshot. In Chapter 8, I will show how to build an RFM score. Here is a formula for producing a quick snapshot score.

Recency, *max score = 20*

Gave in last year	20
Gave 1–2 years ago	15
Gave 2–3 years ago	10
Gave 3–4 years ago	5
Gave 4–5 years ago	2
Gave more than 5 years ago	1
No giving	0

Frequency, *max score = 30*

Frequency% Score

(Gift Count) / [(Last gift year) – (First gift year)]

100%	10 (to be multiplied by years-giving multiplier)
90–99%	8
80–89%	6
70–79%	4
60–69%	2
<60%	1

Years-giving multiplier

20+ years giving	(Frequency % score) * 3.0 = Frequency
15–19 years giving	(Frequency % score) * 2.5 = Frequency
10–14 years giving	(Frequency % score) * 2.0 = Frequency
5–9 years giving	(Frequency % score) * 1.5 = Frequency
<5 years giving	(Frequency % score) * 1 = Frequency
No giving	0 = Frequency score

Monetary Value, max score = 50 (Set gift amounts that make sense for your organization)

$5,000+ outright gift	25
$2,000–$4,999 outright gift	15
$1,000–$1,999 outright gift	10
$500–$999 outright gift	5
<$500	1
No giving	0
$20,000+ cumulative giving	Additional 25
$10,000–$19,999	Additional 15
$5,000–$9,999	Additional 5

RFM Score, max score = 100

Sum of Recency, Frequency, and Monetary Value Scores

Up-selling and Cross-selling

I have a brother who works in business-to-business sales. He will often tell me of his place of employment's incentive programs for up-selling and cross-selling existing customers to secure them for additional products or services. Recently, he won a contest for cross-selling a specific product at his organization. As an incentive, they gave him rinkside tickets to the Minnesota Wild, and he took me with him. This prompted discussion at the game about his company's sales model (while watching the Wild dominate the Oilers).

When his company has a new product or service to offer, they connect with existing, loyal customers first. Not only are these customers more likely to purchase it because of loyalty, but they are also more likely to refer the product to other businesses. A sales professional has to sell the company as well as the product to new customers. For existing customers, they only have to sell the product. The existing customer already has trust in the company.

The focus of annual giving and membership for existing, loyal donors should be on upgrading and cross-promoting. If your donor gives every year to the scholarship campaign, you might ask for an additional gift of unrestricted support or for the new student union initiative. In leadership annual giving programs, you may need to explore specific interests and possible designations to encourage the donor to increase their investment.

Opinion Research

Market research in the corporate world still puts fundraising to shame. However, fundraising holds its own in high-level prospect research. Most companies have a clear picture of the typical customer profile or profiles. They test new products and gather information using surveys and focus groups.

A few sophisticated annual giving and membership programs are connecting with institutional researchers and prospect researchers or building their own market research capacities to study their constituencies. They regularly survey alumni or patients about giving motivations, affinity, or attitudes about the organization in general. Then they design their messages to directly reflect what most resonates with the populations in question.

With the low cost and availability of online surveys, this capacity is more and more accessible for novice researchers. However, there are challenges in online surveys. People now receive so many surveys in their e-mail inbox that they click right by them. It may be difficult to learn from those who don't already view your brand in a positive light. The other challenges come from poor survey design. Novice survey designers will often ask compound questions or have inconsistent answer scales, making the surveys very difficult for both the respondent and the analyst.

Most universities have coursework or speakers to advise about survey design. Many health care and education institutions have existing survey research programs. There should be ample opportunity in many communities to learn solid skills of question-and-answer design.

One basic principle I follow in designing is "start with the end." Determine what you want to know at the end of the survey. Are you looking to segment your file into clusters? Are you looking to test some of the campaign initiatives? Or are you gauging whether attitudes about your organization have improved or deteriorated since last year? Design the survey to answer only the questions you need answered. Your surveys will be more concise. Most people wish they had made the survey shorter when it comes to analyzing the results.

Touch Points

A major component of the customer relationship management movement that was so prevalent in the 1990s was consistent messaging among all touch points. No matter how a customer interacted with a company, he or she would have the same experience: The Web site, the stores, the staff, the advertisements, and so on all presented complementary messages.

I have seen considerably contradictory messages in more organizations than I can count. I will meet with the major giving team and learn of their case for support with clear objectives for the future. They will speak of the vision-oriented messaging highlighting impact and opportunity. Then I will see need-based messaging in an annual fund appeal from the same organization. Even more often, I will see contradictory messaging on the Web site.

If a constituent views a direct mail appeal, goes to the Web site, speaks with gift processing about transaction details, meets with a gift officer, or hears the chief executive make a speech, will they hear consistent messages from your organization?

Geographic Distribution

Thanks to technological developments in geographic information systems, software to map constituents is accessible to even the most novice user. There are desktop applications that allow you to map a basic address file by the country, state, province, county, mailing code, or census tract. Many corporations have divisions dedicated directly to identifying the geographic areas most likely to purchase their products. However, few fundraising organizations are taking advantage of this accessible technology. Geography has a big impact on philanthropy as well.

In health care, you should compare the service area of your care facilities to the areas producing the most donors. In the arts, do your patrons live in your community? Do your major donors live in the same places as your membership at large? Who else lives in the same neighborhood as your major donors? In public universities, I have noticed a great variety of behaviors around campuses. At some universities, the inner rings near the campus neighborhood perform worse as a group than any other areas. At others, this is the strongest segment, with the campus neighborhood showing the weakest performance. They say "Absence makes the heart grow stronger." This definitely seems to be the case in higher education. Faraway alumni seem to have more positive feelings about their institution than nearby alumni, for just about every school I have studied.

TRADITIONAL DONOR SEGMENTS

If you were to take an Annual Giving 101 course, it is likely the first day would center around some very familiar acronyms: LYBUNT and SYBUNT. To an annual giving professional, these terms are second nature. If you are a new analyst, in prospecting, or a major giving professional, these terms are not necessarily familiar. They are basically two of the three primary donor segments. For the sake of the non-annual fund readers, I will define the segments:

1. LYBUNT: Gave last year but unfortunately not this year
2. SYBUNT: Gave some year but unfortunately not this year
3. Never Donors: Never gave a gift to the institution

To help understand the logic of these segments, I like to imagine it is the first day of a new fiscal year and the time is 12:01 A.M. Not a single donor has given to your institution yet. Everyone is a non-donor.

Now, among these non-donors, some gave in the fiscal year you just completed. These are your LYBUNTs. Within the LYBUNTs are those whose gift last year was their first gift ever. These are first-year LYBUNTs. In the first year, most organizations do not ask for increases in gift level. The focus is on sustaining the relationship. Some of the LYBUNTs gave last year and also the year or years before consecutively. These are multi-year LYBUNTs. LYBUNTs remain LYBUNTs until the year ends. If they gave during the new year, they are counted into the renewal rate.

Some of these non-donors did not give last year, but they did the year or two years before that. Basically, they were a LYBUNT last year or the year before. These are your SYBUNTs. Some organizations pull back five years to calculate SYBUNTs, and others only go back three years. If they do go back five years, they usually separate the "Lapsed" from the "Long-lapsed" at the three-year point. If a SYBUNT gives during this fiscal year, they are calculated into the reactivation rate.

The remaining non-donors may have never given a gift, or it has been more than five years. These populations are generally combined into one "Never Donor" pool.

The word "traditional" seems to have a negative connotation in books talking about new technologies. I am not that way. Many of the traditional fundraising practices are tried and true. Peer review and monitoring news alerts are traditional, yet effective, prospecting techniques. The progression from awareness to ownership is a traditional, yet effective, major gift cultivation technique. And the traditional donor segments still provide some of the most effective means of building your annual giving strategies. But these can be stronger when we look within the segments for other characteristics. This has led many annual giving and membership programs to incorporate modeling techniques into their segmentation strategies.

PREDICTIVE MODELING FOR ANNUAL GIVING AND MEMBERSHIP

There are several ways of incorporating predictive modeling into a base development program. In many ways, annual giving and membership have a distinct advantage over major giving in the options available to it.

With the short turnaround time for appeals, models can be tested in a very short timeframe. Major gift models often need a year or more to realize their potential.

The most practical predictive models for annual giving and membership programs are the following:

- Overall likelihood of giving a gift
- Amount of the next gift
- Channel preference models
- Models predicting renewal or reactivation

Overall Likelihood of Giving a Gift

Predicting giving at any level is relatively easy to do because you have so many cases to study. A good analogy might be a digital picture. The more pixels you have in an image, the more clear the picture will be. If you wish to enlarge the picture and you have very few pixels, you will lose clarity. In major giving, there are very few actual major donors in comparison to your file of records. If you hope to apply the characteristics of these few to all of your records, you will have some challenges. In annual giving, since you have so many people who have made a gift to you, applying the picture to the non-donors will be very effective.

I build most of my models for overall giving using regression analysis and decision trees. I describe the mechanics of building a model in Chapter 9 of this book, but I will summarize my approach for building overall giving models here. First, I code all donors to the organization with a variable called "donor" and give them the value "1." All of the non-donors are given a "0" in the donor variable. Next, as described in Chapter 3, I recode and restructure several independent characteristics into numeric variables. Then I use the donor variable as the dependent variable in my statistics software to run the model.

For many health care organizations, there many tribute- and memorial-only donors who should be excluded from the donor variable. They will skew the results away from those who gave in response to annual giving efforts. In higher education, I exclude alumni dues. I leave these populations in only if they have given any other gift. If you are unable to exclude these populations, you may choose to code any constituent with two or more gifts as a donor and use that as your dependent variable.

Overall likelihood models are best applied to your non-donor populations. A way to test the model is to measure the response rate on a "never
donor" mailing. See what the overall response rate is to the mailing, then
determine the response rate by segments of a model you build.

Let's say we had a mailing we sent to 10,000 records. This mailing had
a 10% response rate, with an average gift of $25 per response. Each piece
cost $1.50, and the mailing grossed $25,000. Therefore, the net of the
mailing was $10,000. Now, say we split the file into deciles based on a
likelihood-of-giving model. Then we can see the response rate by each
of the deciles. Look at the table (see facing page).

In this table, it appears that if we had mailed to the top 70% of the file,
our net would have been $3,000 higher than mailing to the entire file. In
this example, all of the segments averaged $25 per gift. It is likely your
gift amounts will also be higher in the top deciles. Even in this math-
friendly example, the bottom 30% of the file actually *lost* money.

Amount of the Next Gift

I have run many regression models predicting the amount a person might
give for their next gift. In these models, if the dollar amount from the
regression formula is higher than the scheduled increase, I would recommend asking for two levels' increase instead of one. If the dollar level is
below existing performance, I would recommend asking for one step
above the individual's current behavior. If the donor shows a very significant potential for high-dollar giving, I would encourage assigning the
donor for leadership of annual giving departments to pursue a personal
visit, or I would send the name to prospect research.

To build this model, I begin by determining my dependent variable.
I have used a variety of dependent variables, including most recent gift
given, largest gift given, or a forecasted gift from a trend line. Very frequently, I will combine them. For example, I have had good success taking the mean of the most recent gift and the largest gift amount. Since I
use a linear regression model, I use the actual dollar amount as the
dependent variable. If there are some conspicuous outliers (really big
gifts), I might scrub them out. If your application is to annual giving, it
will be okay to control for the major donors. Then I will use many independent characteristics, including other linear variables such as capacity,

Decile	Cumulative Count	Responses	Response Rate	Cumulative Response Rate	Dollars by Segment	Net at $1.50 Piece	Cumulative Net
1	1,000	190	19.0%	19.0%	$4,750	$3,250	3,250
2	2,000	180	18.0%	18.5%	$4,500	$3,000	6,250
3	3,000	155	15.5%	17.5%	$3,875	$2,375	8,625
4	4,000	125	12.5%	16.3%	$3,125	$1,625	10,250
5	5,000	120	12.0%	15.4%	$3,000	$1,500	11,750
6	6,000	105	10.5%	14.6%	$2,625	$1,125	12,875
7	7,000	65	6.5%	13.4%	$1,625	$125	**13,000**
8	8,000	45	4.5%	12.3%	$1,125	–$375	12,625
9	9,000	10	1.0%	11.1%	$250	–$1,250	11,375
10	10,000	5	0.5%	10.0%	$125	–$1,375	10,000

age, or RFM data. After the model produces a predicted next gift, I will recode the variable into ranges matching the gift level breakpoints.

Channel Preference Models

Most annual giving and membership programs have multiple channels for soliciting gifts. The most common are direct mail, phone, online, and personal solicitations. Part of incorporating analytics into your annual giving strategies is determining the best channel for each constituent. The most affordable channel is the right channel. I have seen organizations send direct mail appeals four times a year to constituents who only ever give to telemarketing. If they only give by phone, why send the letter?

One method I use frequently to determine the best channel is discriminant modeling. I code all donors who give by each channel with a number indicating that channel. I may also code all donors by the channel that produces the largest RFM score or produces the largest overall giving amounts. I make this number code the range in my discriminant model. Then I include several independent characteristics, as outlined in Chapter 3. The outcome of this model is the most likely channel for successful future solicitations.

Beyond Predictive Modeling

Having in-house analytics capacity will enable your annual fund to run some pretty powerful models for each appeal and initiative. In addition, many of the programs investing in analytics have found the skill sets to be valuable in other areas as well.

The analysts trained with the statistical tools to build the models will be able to ask questions of the data and find answers really quickly. They can test the impact of alumni activities on response rates to determine timing for drops. They can determine if it is worthwhile to segment by generations. Using statistical software, they can very quickly calculate the difference in renewal between your first-year LYBUNTs and all other LYBUNTs, and the reporting of progress toward goals is made much simpler.

An additional by-product of building analytics capacity is the opportunities it provides to work with other departments and units. I have seen wonderful partnerships grow between institutional research programs, admissions programs, annual fund strategies, and prospecting analysts. These partnerships would help your organization better tap into the multidimensional relationships your constituents have with your organizations.

METRICS FOR ANNUAL GIVING

When I described how to determine metrics for your prospect management program in Chapter 5, I started by emphasizing the need to evaluate your business process first. After you have a firm understanding of the objectives of your program, you will be able to determine the metrics that best help you measure and achieve your goals. This same process works for annual giving as well. Here are some of the primary objectives within your goals of broadening the base and building sustained giving relationships:

- Acquire new donors for the organization
- Engage non-donor constituents with giving relationships
- Renew previous-year donors
- Reactivate lapsed donors
- Upgrade donors' giving levels
- Move donors into the major giving pipeline
- With leadership annual giving programs, maximize gift officer yields and qualify new prospects

Following are some metrics according to each of the primary objectives to consider as you work to improve your annual giving and membership program.

Acquire New Donors for the Organization

- Return on investment for list acquisition
- Total number of new donors per year
- New donors acquired by geo-demographic segments, such as generation, location, graduation year, patients, etc.
- Numbers of new donors by sources, including list acquisition and natural constituencies
- Success rates of each appeal and channel type, including phone, letter, postcard, e-mail, emotion-based appeals, appeals highlighting the case for support, appeals to logic using facts and figures, etc.
- The projected lifetime value of new donors

Engage Non-Donor Constituents with Giving Relationships

- Activation rates by area of connection, including alumni, athletics attendees, fine arts participants, museum visitors, lecture attendees, community events, patients, families, etc.
- The effectiveness of predictive models on identification (participation by score)
- Times of year when donors are most effectively acquired overall and by connection types

Renew Previous-Year Donors

- The overall renewal rate, with corresponding average gifts, total dollars raised, and total number of donors
- Renewal rates of first-year LYBUNTs and multiyear LYBUNTs, with corresponding average gifts, total dollars raised, and total number of donors
- Sources of acquired names producing best renewal statistics
- Cost to renew a donor, compared to the cost to acquire a new donor
- Times of year when LYBUNTs are most effectively renewed, overall and by connection types

Reactivate Lapsed Donors

- Three-year SYBUNT reactivation rate, with corresponding average gifts, total dollars raised, and total number of donors
- Five-year SYBUNT reactivation rate, with corresponding average gifts, total dollars raised, and total number of donors
- Cost to reactivate a SYBUNT compared to the cost to acquire a new donor
- Cost to reactivate a SYBUNT compared to the cost to renew a LYBUNT
- Times of year when SYBUNTs are most effectively acquired, overall and by connection types
- When SYBUNTs reactivate most often, in relation to campus events, arts activities, economic factors, etc.

Upgrade Donors' Giving Levels

- Count and percentage of donors upgrading per year
- Total dollars and average gifts from upgrades alone

- First-year, multiyear, and overall LYBUNT average renewal gift amounts, total dollars, and whether asking for upgrades in first year or not
- Upgrade comparison by channel (Do donors upgrade better by phone than by mail?)
- Effect of ask amount models on upgrades when compared to a control group

Move Donors into the Major Giving Pipeline

- Total count of prospects produced by year
- Annual giving dollars received from prospects when under management
- Total dollars received per year produced by prospects identified or engaged through the annual fund

Engaging Leadership Annual Giving Prospects

- Percentage of capacity acquired by gift officer portfolio
- Target ask amounts compared to capacity, overall and by manager portfolio
- Actual ask amounts compared to the target amounts, overall and by manager portfolio
- Gifts received compared to the ask amounts, overall and by manager portfolio
- Gifts received compared to the original capacity or next give amount model, overall and by manager portfolio
- Total dollars raised by the program and by each officer
- Total visits by the program and by each officer
- Total number of discovery calls made and percent of suspects qualified for the major gift program
- Total number of assists (handoffs to major giving staff)
- Total dollars produced by handoffs

FINAL THOUGHTS ON ANNUAL GIVING ANALYTICS

Many annual giving and membership staff members feel as if they are second-class citizens in their fundraising program. They see the large dollar amounts produced by major giving. In some organizations, major giving staffs earn much higher salaries than annual giving staffs. This is changing.

To run an effective annual giving or membership program, professionals need to acquire a much more sophisticated arsenal of analytical techniques. It requires skills that are not easily found in the industry. With the high levels of turnover in base development staffing and the increasing needs of organizations for solid annual giving and membership programs, qualified professionals are in high demand. In economic terms, when demand increases, prices increase, and several organizations are paying much higher salaries to keep and retain good staff.

The key to becoming an in-demand annual giving and membership professional rests in building your analytics capacity. Numbers drive annual funds. Those large major giving dollar amounts would not be there if you did not start that relationship. You need to be equipped to show the impact of your program, and you need to understand the factors that make your program successful. You need to know the numbers.

CHAPTER 7

Selecting Data for Mining

When I speak around the country about data mining, I invariably get asked, "What are the top variables for predicting major giving?" Answering this question goes against a fundamental component of data mining. In data mining, the idea is to have the computer software find the patterns in your data. The question also poses another issue: Do we really want to predict major giving?

On the surface, the answer seems an obvious yes. But what is the actual goal of your model? It is more likely to find *new* people who might give a major gift. In fraud detection, the most predictive variable is committing fraud in the past. If you wrote a bad check in the past, you are likely to write a bad check again. If you paid off several loans on time without any late payments, you are likely to pay the next loan off in the same manner. In major giving, if you have a major gift in the past, you are likely to give another one. If you were to deliver a list of current major donors to your prospect research team as the best prospects for the next campaign, they would say, "Thanks for nothing! We already know about them."

If you are looking for patterns to identify prospects, predict first-time donors, or predict new season ticket subscribers, it is in your best interest to start big with your file, so you have many potential points of comparison. I am very willing to have a model with several variables if it means I can identify a few more prospects. Many statisticians will try and refine the model to six to eight really good variables that apply to many people. You should be willing to expect some variables that will apply to your major and planned donors but do not apply to many people.

Over the next several pages, I will walk through a very comprehensive list of data points I might use as I build my initial dataset for predictive modeling and analysis projects.

SELECTION CRITERIA

It is critical that all models you build are in a random environment. If you recall the hat analogy in Chapter 3, you will remember the goal was to pull major donor slips at a greater frequency than random by using the independent characteristics of shapes, sizes, and color. If you select a pool based on criteria, you have already hindered your modeling potential.

My preferred selection is all records. I will separate individuals from organizations, because the data is so different between them. It is as if you are working with two databases. I may or may not include deceased records, depending on my analysis. If I were looking at overall giving by year, and I excluded deceased records, I would end up excluding the dollars the constituents gave while they were alive. If I am looking for the characteristics of surprise bequests, I have no choice but to include the deceased. If you do include deceased records in your data query, be sure to provide an indicator variable so they might be identified.

If you are working in a flat file environment, which I generally do because of the nature of working with several clients, the scale of your file might be an issue. If you are in higher education or the arts, it is doubtful that your entire database is beyond the capacity of leading statistics software products. The largest universities rarely have more than 1 million to 1.5 million records in their entire database. That is a workable amount. Some health care and membership organizations with long histories of high-volume direct mail will have many millions of records. I have built models on 5 million– to 6 million–record flat files, and could score a flat file. When my record counts get into the millions, I will often pull random samples to build my final model. Then I will bring in all of the records to apply the score.

VARIABLES TO INCLUDE IN YOUR FILE

Giving Data

For some models and forecasts, you will use giving fields as independent variables. In most models, you will use the giving fields to define your dependent variables or what you are trying to predict or describe. Following are some of the giving fields I have used in my models.

Lifetime Cumulative Giving   This is the total amount a person or organization has given in their lifetime. I prefer to use hard credit data so I can aggregate the total giving of all records and get a true picture of the total amount raised by the constituency. This variable might be used as a dependent characteristic for lifetime value models. However, it is better to review gifts over time in relation to inflation for understanding lifetime value.

Total Gift Count   The total distinct count of hard credit and also soft credit gifts can be informative for many types of models and analysis. It is a common variable to use in RFM analysis. Additionally, it will enable you to calculate the average number of gifts for all donors, as well as donors by level. Some planned giving models also incorporate gift count. I often build models for planned giving while holding back the impact of gift count and age. I do this because many planned giving programs already use this as targeting criteria, and I am looking for new potential predictive factors for planned giving. It is better to exclude alumni dues and distinct payroll deductions or electronic funds transfers. When an individual chooses an automatic payment method, it is more like one gift with many payments than it is many gifts. They made one choice to give.

EFT Giving   Gifts made by electronic funds transfer might be separated from other giving. As many organizations build this very effective capacity for sustaining consecutive donors, they may choose to model the behavior and expand the participation pool. This model might use an EFT donor as the dependent variable and study the characteristics to find others who fit the EFT profile. By targeting segments more amenable to alternate payment options with EFT messages, you may be able to more efficiently increase this method of giving.

Total of All Planned Gifts   I recommend extracting one field with the total dollars of all planned gifts, whether realized or expected. I might also pull out gifts by specific vehicle, such as bequests, trusts, or annuities. If you are building a planned giving model, you might make a binary-dependent variable indicating any constituent with any dollar amount in this field. You might also separate planned gifts by level, realized gifts from expected, or have separate dependent variables for each vehicle type.

Planned Giving Society   Many fundraising organizations have planned giving or "heritage" societies for all donors who have made planned gifts or say they have made planned gifts. Even though this might be coded as an attribute, it is really a giving field. It might be an ideal field to use as a dependent variable if you have difficulty pulling your expected planned gifts.

Largest Outright Gift   The largest outright gift field is populated with the value indicating the largest amount of money ever given to the organization in a single transaction. This field and the largest pledge amount are the most important data points for building a major giving model. If you define a major gift as a combination of an outright gift of $5,000 or a pledge of $25,000, this field enables you to derive the donors of $5,000 outright. In major giving models, I am most interested in the *choice* to make a major gift. Because of this, I will pull soft credit as well as hard credit data for the largest gift amount. If you wanted to know how many donors had ever given gifts of $1 million, $100,000, or $25,000, this field would enable you to count that very quickly in your statistics software.

Largest Pledge   The largest pledge is the largest amount a person has ever *committed* to give to an organization. I might combine the largest gift amount with the largest pledge amount in one field, depending on the model in question.

Most Recent Gift or Pledge Amount   If you are evaluating constituent value or building next-gift amount models, it will be necessary to extract the amount of the most recent gift transaction on file. Often, I will compare this gift amount to the average of preceding gifts to look for springboard activity. Sudden spikes in gift amounts in comparison to gift history and regardless of level are enormously predictive of major giving propensity.

Date of Most Recent Gift or Pledge   To build an RFM analysis of your constituency, you will need to extract the actual date of the most recent gift or pledge. Depending on how specific your analysis may or may not be, you might choose to extract only the most recent fiscal year. When measuring an entire database, the fiscal year is often sufficient as a data point.

First Gift Amount The amount of the first gift given to an organization has a strong correlation to major giving. Even when you control for donors who gave their first gifts at the major or high mid-range levels, you will see this correlation at most institutions. In other words, if your first gift was $100, you may be somewhat more likely to give a major gift than if your first gift was $50.

First Gift Date The date the first gift was ever given to an institution is necessary to calculate the longevity of the giving relationship. In RFM analysis and planned giving models, this variable factors greatly. I often use the date and time wizard in SPSS (Statistical Package for the Social Sciences software) to quickly calculate the amount of time between the first gift date and the most recent gift date. Then I might create a ranking of longevity (generally quintiles or deciles) to use as an ordinal independent variable.

First Major Gift Date I rarely pull this field except for some very specific major giving models. It simply lists the date a person first reaches the organizational definition of a major gift donor. When I use this variable, I calculate the distance between first gift and first major gift. Then I build a model predicting the amount of time it might take to become a major donor. In some cases, I compare the first major gift date to the date a donor was first assigned to a manager. Then I might take a descriptive look at the differences in average times to major gift by each officer.

Giving by Fiscal Year If you are conducting campaign analysis or projecting annual giving totals, you would pull the total hard credit amount given by each constituent in a fiscal year. I typically include data from at least the last five years. I prefer to have 10 or more years for most projects. In your projection models, you might split this at a dollar amount for separate forecast types. For example, your gifts under $25,000 might be more predictable and follow a linear trend line. You may need to try other approaches for gifts above $25,000, if they even can be forecasted with confidence.

Annual Fund or Membership Gifts by Fiscal Year   To analyze an annual fund or membership program and produce the giving segments, you will need to extract the giving specifically counted towards your annual fund or membership programs. If you hope to calculate five years of SYBUNTs, you must pull at least eight years of annual giving numbers.

Giving by Month   The only times I pull gift amounts down to the month level are when I am evaluating the timing of annual giving appeals or making very specific giving forecasts. A simple and quick way to analyze this monthly giving is to plot the sum of annual gifts by month on a line graph, then mark the dates of various activities or events on this same graph. As with forecast models, I separate the major-level gifts from all other gifts when looking at monthly giving.

Matching Gifts   Occasionally, I have used constituents with matching gift companies as characteristic in my model. More often, I use it for descriptive means when studying a segment.

Channel   To build channel preference models, or to evaluate your annual fund, you will need to analyze giving by channel (mail, phone, online, in-person, and other). In annual giving analysis, I pull this data for every year, going back at least five years. For channel preference modeling, I might only pull the total by each channel.

Constituent Types

I always pull all of the primary constituent types in my modeling and analysis projects. You should know the percentages of your dollars and donors that come from patients, alumni, friends, members, parents, etc. off the top of your head.

Individual Record   For most of your predictive models, you will need to separate individuals from organizations. This flag will be necessary for filtering the file. If your only goal is to use the dataset for predictive models on individuals, you would include it as a selection criteria and ignore the organization constituent types.

Foundation Record Depending on your analysis, you may want to separate family foundations from other grantmaking foundations. Corporate foundations are usually counted as corporation records.

Corporation Record If you have an entire database extraction, it will be important to watch hard credit versus soft credit when including corporation records. If you have corporations linked to individuals, the very big employers might be an independent variable by themselves.

Alumni Status Include all graduates with the alumni field. Be aware that alumni will often have negative correlations to giving in random populations. This is because all alumni will be entered on your system. Non-alumni are entered on your system disproportionately because they gave a gift to your organization. If the whole state or province was your database, being an alumni would be among the strongest positive correlations you had.

Attendee Status The non-graduating attendees are a surprisingly strong segment in some models. Do not exclude this demographic.

Alumni Association Membership If all alumni are automatically entered into the alumni association, it does not make sense to pull this field. Also, be sure to keep dues separate from other gifts.

Parents Parents will often be good prospects for student life projects, such as residences, unions, libraries, etc., as long as the project will benefit their children. Many colleges screen the freshman parents for wealth data every year so they can maximize relationship building with the most likely prospects.

Faculty Many fundraising organizations ignore their faculty. Do not do this. They are frequently strong performers in planned giving models.

Staff Staff are also ignored by most organizations. I always include them; however, they perform less well than doctors or faculty.

Patient   If you do not have your patient file linked to your fundraising database, take care of this. Begin a strategy to link these data sources to your files. It might take time, but there is no time like the present. There is no doubt that the patient relationship and the patient family relationship are key elements of a model.

Demographics

Several demographics data points can be purchased to enhance your file. These include the fields listed below. Some consumer behavior data can be helpful, as well. I have had some models where certain magazine subscriptions fared better than others. Additionally, people who buy many things often give less.

Deceased   If you include all records in your file, be sure to remember your deceased flag.

Birth Year   Age almost always factors into models. I will generally recode this variable into buckets by generations or decades for analysis.

Marital Status   Married people give more than unmarried people. At the same time, some of the other marital codes perform well in some models. Lifelong single people, for example, are consistent planned-giving donors.

Presence of Children   The stage of life where children are present usually coincides with limited financial giving. However, as the children age and move out of the house, the parents will become interested in volunteer opportunities. This is not true across the board, but I have seen some compelling correlations.

Level of Education   For nonacademic educations, level of education is correlated with wealth and capacity. This information is worth acquiring in surveys or testing a data enhancement.

Gender   I generally do not pull gender except for special initiatives. I find it rarely predictive for general models. The relationship usually points out the historic practice of coding the husband over the wife on joint gifts.

Contact Information and Restrictions

For descriptive and annual giving analysis, you should always include contact information and restrictions. Occasionally, these variables make good independent variables as well.

Address Status   Include an indicator for a good mailing address.

Phone Status   Include an indicator for a good phone number.

E-mail Status   If you are profiling a segment, it is helpful to know how many are reachable by e-mail. In the late 1990s, I found the e-mail extension (.com, .edu, .net, .org) to have interesting relationships to giving. This may be the case for you as well.

Multiple Home Addresses   Owning multiple homes is a consistent performer in many major and planned gift models.

Business Address Status   Very often, major donors will only give you their business address. Presence of a business address is a good variable. The business address as the preferred address is even stronger.

Do Not Contact/Mail/Phone/Etc.   I always test restrictions against giving by those channels when I have the opportunity. These codes are notorious for being dated.

Geography

There are numerous methods of segmenting your file by geography. If I had to choose one, I would use the ZIP or mailing code, which provides the most flexibility.

State   In modeling, restructure your state variable into separate 1/0 variables so you can test each state against giving.

ZIP Code I use residence for ZIP code when I have it, then I go to preferred, then I go to business. You can break it up by digits to expand the regions. A three-digit ZIP code is one of the most useful cuts.

Country For some nonprofits, this data point is important. Many organizations do not maintain their foreign records as well as their domestic records. Remember this if your foreign records score poorly. It might be a matter of missing data.

Metropolitan Statistical Area Some organizations maintain the MSA code. It is useful if you have it.

Area Code The phone area code is a geographic indicator you may overlook.

Academics

Educational institutions can tap into a wide variety of data points in their academic records. Here are some of the primary fields I pull into my data files.

Year of First Degree I calculate graduation years from the first degree field. Most donors give to their first college academic experience over the other academic experiences.

First College For universities, you should pull the school attended within the university.

First Department or Major For undergraduates, the academic major connects students more than any other factor, other than year of graduation.

Multiple Degrees Occasionally, multiple degree holders score well in giving models. However, it is less often than you might expect for most organizations.

Undergraduate/Graduate Degree Holder Remember to include a flag for undergraduate and graduate students.

Advisor   For graduate students, the graduate advisor connects them to other students more than any other factor.

Employment

Employment information is among the most useful for most predictive models. If you do not have strategies for capturing employment information, you should think about it. It enables you to segment by industry sector, infer wealth, connect peers, and secure matching gifts.

Job Title   The job title is among the most useful fields for prospect research. Executive, educator, government, and professional classifications of job titles are consistent factors for major- and planned-gift models.

Employer   The leading employers for your constituents might be good independent variables.

SIC   The Standard Industrial Classification (SIC) codes enable you to group companies by industry. Very few of my clients have had this available, but it has been useful when it is there.

Retired   The retired flag has influenced more than just planned giving models. I have used it in major giving, annual giving, and channel preference models.

Participation

Data that describes nongiving involvement can prove to be the best data. You should be ever vigilant about opportunities to capture names from campus activities, health events, or arts programs.

Member of Any Institutional Boards   Board involvement is among the most related to giving major gifts. Do you have the members of all boards at your organization coded in your database?

Current or Previous Trustee   Most descriptive analysis projects of program performance will highlight the performance of the primary governing board. It is too small and too closely tied to major giving to use as an effective independent variable.

Received Any Institutional Awards   Sometimes award recipients score really well in models. They are not as strong performers as most organizations hope.

Responded to Any Constituent or Alumni Surveys   Survey responsiveness is one of the best predictors of direct-mail responsiveness.

Event Count   Event data almost always shows up in giving models. It is most effective if you can isolate out the fundraising events from the non-fundraising events. Fundraising event data should not be used to predict giving.

Athletics Season Ticket Holders   Similar to the patient database in health care, many universities have difficulty connecting their fundraising database with the athletics ticketing office. If you have it available, it is very worthwhile to include this information in your data file.

Fine Arts Attendance   Many fine arts events in education are free events. Some are free with registration. This provides an opportunity to capture names at events. In arts organizations, you have the opportunity to pull attendance by genre, multiple attendance, package subscriptions, and so forth.

Clubs or Organizations   Any code that groups constituents together because of a social activity or event is worth evaluation.

Scholarship Recipients   Recipients of scholarships sometimes make good scholarship donors as well. Connecting recipients with the donors of those scholarships is good stewardship practice. It can also be excellent cultivation of the recipient. Test this data over time.

Volunteered at the Hospital   Hospital volunteers, outside of boards and advisory groups, are often overlooked. Do not assume there is not wealth there.

Visited the Web Site   For obvious reasons, Web activity is predictive of online giving. It also may give you indications of topical interests.

Opened an Online Newsletter   Opening an online newsletter shows a constituent is Web-responsive. Clicking through on stories aligned to your campaign priorities will indicate potential interests.

Called in a Complaint   Constituents who call to complain are not necessarily negatively correlated with giving. In fact, in public broadcasting, these individuals give at a higher level than random. If you are not invested in a public broadcasting station and you see something that bothers you, you change the channel. If you care, you call.

Student Activities

The level of participation as a student is very similar to the level of participation as an alumnus. I have even seen high school participation data correlate positively with college alumni participation at a couple schools. Below are some of the most commonly available student activity data points.

Fraternities or Sororities   Greek membership usually has an impact on annual giving models. Occasionally, it will show up in major and planned giving models as well. Greek segments can be effectively filtered using peer review by class years.

Athletics   Intercollegiate athletics participation tends to be too small a field to include in most models except those benefiting the athletics programs directly.

Intramural Athletics   Very few schools capture intramural athletics. It has always had a modest, positive correlation with giving. Beyond that, it might not be worth the effort to extract.

Relationships   For planned giving models, number of family relationships is right up there with consistent giving and age as a consistent factor. Do all you can to capture family, peer, professional, and organizational relationships. This is solid data.

Patient Data

There are many HIPAA-compliant data sources for patient information. The biggest challenge for most medical centers is linking the databases. Here are a few recommended fields I have used in data mining projects.

Spouse of Patient   By far, spouse of a patient is the strongest patient data field. It frequently outperforms the surviving patient data field as a donor of major gifts. Other family relationships, such as grandparents or children, are also worth evaluation if possible.

Count of Patient Visits   This is the total count of visits to the hospital or care facility.

Count of Visits with a Physician   This is the total count of visits where the patient saw any physician.

Last Patient Date   It is a helpful exercise to compare dates of giving to the last patient visit date.

First Patient Date   The first patient date behaves much like graduation year, because there is a short window to engage the patient after their first visit. If you look back at your first gift dates in comparison to first patient date, I expect you will see strong numbers in the first two years, with a dramatic decline after that.

Method of Payment/Financial Class   This field indicates whether the person paid out of pocket, was insured by an HMO, received assistance, or so forth.

Interests

I recommend categorizing all of the interests relating to your mission into broad categories and including interest grids on your constituent surveys (health/fitness, books/learning, fine arts, etc.). You might also derive interests through the prospect research and field qualification process. Here is a list of common interests:

- Science
- Fine arts

- Athletics
- Capital needs
- Scholarships
- Research
- Programs
- Youth and family
- Justice and equality
- Professorships
- Endowment
- Health and fitness
- Spirituality
- Student life

If you have interest attributes, always include them in your initial data files for review. If interest data consistently underperforms, simply exclude them from future extracts. If the data performs well, consider enhancing your data file with purchased data.

Prospect Development

Most prospect management data would only be used in descriptive analysis and pipeline forecasting. However, after you build predictive models, it is good to evaluate the results against current efforts. Here is a list of the prospect management fields I like to include in my analysis:

- Managed prospects
- Prospect managers by name
- Capacity rating
- Any existing affinity or propensity ratings
- Target ask amount
- Target ask date
- Number of personal visits
- Contact report count
- Prospect management classification
- Prospect management stage
- Researched record
- Submitted proposals
- Funded proposals

Wealth Screening

To conduct a composite capacity analysis as described in Chapter 4, you should extract all of the wealth indicators available to you for evaluation. Then you can apply a formula to all of the indicators to estimate capacity. The following list of screening and asset data is the most commonly available in fundraising databases:

- Total dollar amount of all securities (directly held)
- Total sales of private company
- Total dollar amount of private company valuations
- Total value of real estate
- Wealth codes from banking and finance source
- Total foundation assets
- Total amount of other assets, including luxury items such as art, yachts, and aircraft
- Total income
- Total identified assets amount
- Net worth from a publication
- Contributions to other charities
- Political giving as recorded by the FEC

FORMAT FOR YOUR DATA FILE

In most statistics software, it is easy to convert the formats of data between string and text fields. For predictive modeling projects, you will end up converting most of your variables into numeric fields. If it is possible to extract the data in that format, it will save you considerable time. For yes/no attributes, simply extract them as 1/0 fields, in which 1 = yes and 0 = no.

Most software programs are able to import files of various types as well. SPSS, for example, can open CSV, tab-delimited text, Microsoft Excel®, SAS, and other standard file types. My personal preference for ease of import is tab-delimited text.

CHAPTER 8

Descriptive Analysis: Basic Statistics and Scoring Models

Over the next pages, I will show you how to run some of the very basic statistical operations you might use to analyze a constituent file. It is by no means a course in statistics. Entire textbooks are devoted to the math behind many of these operations. Although I will use some statistics terms and operations, I needed to abbreviate some of the explanations to focus on mechanics. Throughout these how-to sections, I will demonstrate using SPSS (Statistical Package for the Social Sciences) software screen prints. There are several excellent statistical software products on the market you can use to do this same analysis.

I use SPSS for several reasons. First, my background in fundraising before becoming a data mining consultant was in the academic setting. SPSS is very prevalent at universities and colleges, and I was able to get support and meet with other SPSS users. Second, I found SPSS to be very user-friendly for novices while still being very powerful for advanced users. It serves as a versatile training product at a variety of institutions. Third, I found many fundraising staff members had backgrounds in the social sciences. Many sociology, political science, psychology, geography, statistics, and economics programs have statistical analysis components. I found the majority of people I spoke to from these fields used SPSS for their undergraduate and graduate projects. Because of this existing working knowledge, they are able to pick up analytics techniques very quickly.

Although I will demonstrate many techniques using SPSS software, this is not a comprehensive how-to guide for using SPSS. Instead, I will focus on key instructions for running analysis of fundraising files. There are several courses and texts providing comprehensive instructions for using the software. For any statistics software you choose to use, I recommend taking a classroom course or online seminar to learn the basics. Most software companies offer these. Also, many professional development training centers, universities, and colleges also offer basic statistics and statistics software learning opportunities.

DESCRIPTIVES

Among the most common statistics you will run are the basic descriptives. These are your sums, means, medians, modes, counts, minimums, maximums, and so forth. Most people have a basic knowledge of descriptive statistics. They may understand the basic definitions, but not how to calculate them.

Sum

A sum is simply a total of values. To calculate the total dollars ever given to your institution using statistics software, you would calculate the sum of a total lifetime giving variable for each constituent.

To calculate a sum in SPSS, select Analyze > Descriptive Statistics > Descriptives (Exhibit 8.1).

Select the "Lifetime_Giving" variable, move it into the "Variable(s)" box, and click the "Options" button (Exhibit 8.2).

Check the box next to the word "Sum" and click "Continue" (Exhibit 8.3).

Now click the "OK" button. A new window will open with your output (Exhibit 8.4). It will contain the count of records and the number of these with valid data (not null). Then, it will contain the sum of your lifetime giving in the file.

Averages

The mean is the average of all of the cases. If you divided the sum by the count of records, your would get the mean. You should decide whether your goal is to calculate the average gift of all of your constituents or just the donors. If you are looking for the average gift by donors, you must

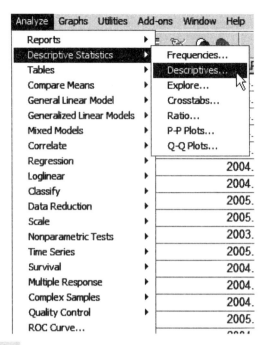

EXHIBIT 8.1   ANALYZE > DESCRIPTIVE STATISTICS > DESCRIPTIVES

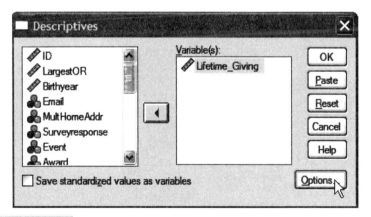

EXHIBIT 8.2   DESCRIPTIVES DIALOGUE BOX

change "$0" giving totals to null values. I will explain how to do this later in the chapter, when we recode variables. In SPSS, simply follow the same process as calculating the sum, except select the "Mean" check box. Your result will look like Exhibit 8.5.

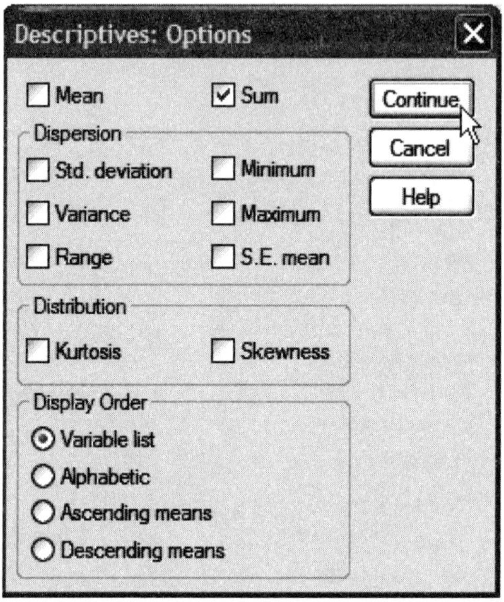

EXHIBIT 8.3   DESCRIPTIVES OPTIONS

	N	Sum
Lifetime_Giving	50000	$44,848,939
Valid N (listwise)	50000	

EXHIBIT 8.4   DESCRIPTIVES OUTPUT: SUM

	N	Mean
Lifetime_Giving	50000	$896.97
Valid N (listwise)	50000	

EXHIBIT 8.5   DESCRIPTIVES OUTPUT: MEAN INCLUDING NON-DONORS

	N	Mean
Lifetime_Giving	21641	$2072.40
Valid N (listwise)	21641	

EXHIBIT 8.6   DESCRIPTIVES OUTPUT: MEAN INCLUDING NON-DONORS

If you changed your zeros to null values, it might look like Exhibit 8.6.

As you can see, several of these basic statistics are incorporated into the "Descriptive Statistics" dialogue box. However, some of the measurements of central tendency, such as the median and the mode, are not included here. The median is the point where there are an equal number of gifts greater and less than the amount. The mode is the most recurring value. One way to calculate these is to use the "Frequencies" operation. Another way is to use the Custom Tables function (if you have the Tables module).

To calculate this using the "Frequencies" operation, Select Analyze > Descriptive Statistics > Frequencies and select your variable. Next, click the "Statistics" button. Here you will see the options for median and mode (Exhibit 8.7). Check these boxes and click to continue.

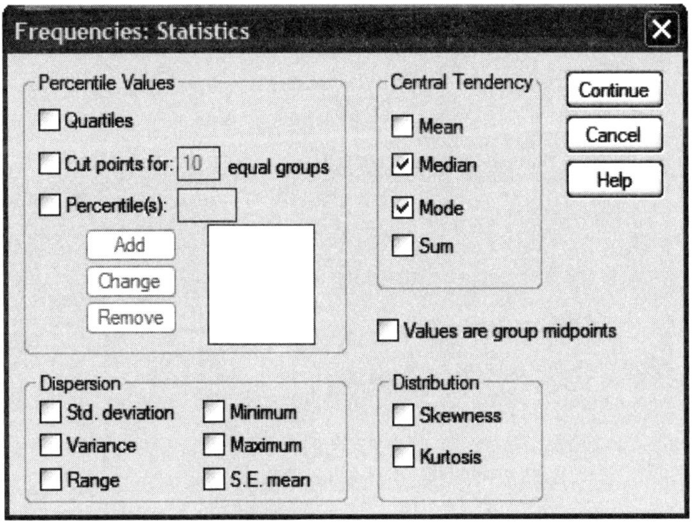

EXHIBIT 8.7   FREQUENCY STATISTICS DIALOGUE BOX

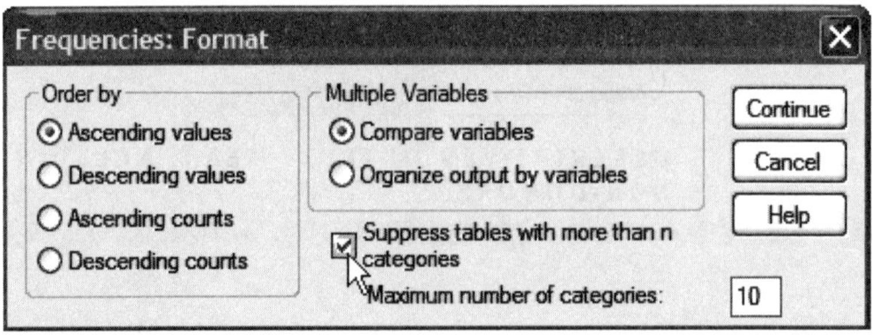

EXHIBIT 8.8   **FREQUENCY FORMAT DIALOGUE BOX**

When calculating frequency statistics on a large-scale variable, you will want to keep it from producing an actual frequency distribution, which is covered in the next section. Instead, you just want the statistics. To prevent it from calculating the entire frequency distribution, click the "Format" button, then select the option to "Suppress tables with more than *n* categories" (Exhibit 8.8).

Click to continue and then click "OK". Exhibit 8.9 shows your output.

In this file of 50,000 records, there are 21,641 donors and 28,359 non-donors. The 21,641 donors have given $44,848,939 over their lifetimes. The average of gifts given was $2,072. The median of gifts given was $90, which indicates there is one or several very large gifts bringing up the mean. The most common gift amount is $25.

This is a lot of information to produce from a few short clicks. You will find, as you use statistics software, that calculations that took some time or were beyond the limits of spreadsheet software have become very possible to run in a short amount of time.

Lifetime_Giving

N	Valid	21641
	Missing	28359
Median		90.00
Mode		25.00

EXHIBIT 8.9   **FREQUENCY STATISTICS OUTPUT**

FREQUENCY DISTRIBUTION

In database management, each individual or corporation has a record assigned to them. In statistics, the common term is *case*. If you wanted to know how many records on your database were married, you might run a SQL function to calculate the count. In statistics, you might phrase the operation slightly differently. You might say, "What is the frequency of 'M' occurring among my cases?" To find the values within a field, you would run a *frequency distribution*.

To calculate a frequency distribution in SPSS, select Analyze > Descriptive Statistics > Frequencies. If the dialogue box is already populated, simply click the "Reset" button. Now, select your variable. In this case, we will select the "Marital Status" variable. After you click "OK", you will see the following output (Exhibit 8.10).

Each value within the marital status field has a frequency, percent, valid percent, and a cumulative percent. The frequency is the count. The percent is the percentage of the file having that value. The valid percent shows the percentage of valid cases. If you had null values, this percentage would be different from the overall percentage. The cumulative percent cumulates the percentage as you go down the list in order. For larger lists, you may wish to see the top frequencies in a field. To do this, you need to list the values by descending counts. Repeat the process to produce your frequency distribution. Before you click "OK", click the

		Frequency	Percent	Valid Percent	Cumulative Percent
Valid	Divorced	142	.3	.3	.3
	Domestic Partne	198	.4	.4	.7
	Formerly marrie	7	.0	.0	.7
	Married	18246	36.5	36.5	37.2
	Separated	16	.0	.0	37.2
	Single	4021	8.0	8.0	45.3
	Unknown Marital	27037	54.1	54.1	99.3
	Widowed	333	.7	.7	100.0
	Total	50000	100.0	100.0	

EXHIBIT 8.10   **FREQUENCY DISTRIBUTION SORTED BY ASCENDING VALUES**

		Frequency	Percent	Valid Percent	Cumulative Percent
Valid	Unknown Marital	27037	54.1	54.1	54.1
	Married	18246	36.5	36.5	90.6
	Single	4021	8.0	8.0	98.6
	Widowed	333	.7	.7	99.3
	Domestic Partne	198	.4	.4	99.7
	Divorced	142	.3	.3	100.0
	Separated	16	.0	.0	100.0
	Formerly marrie	7	.0	.0	100.0
	Total	50000	100.0	100.0	

EXHIBIT 8.11   FREQUENCY DISTRIBUTION SORTED BY DESCENDING COUNTS

"Format" button. Then select "Descending Counts". This time, the output returns the same values sorted by descending counts (Exhibit 8.11).

When I load a new file into SPSS, I will run a snapshot quality-control check of all of my fields. By seeing the basic statistics of all my scale variables and frequencies for all of my categorical and ordinal variables, I can quickly assess whether there are issues with the file.

To run a large quality-control check using SPSS, open the frequencies dialogue box. Click all of the fields into the "Variable(s)" space. Then click the "Format" box to sort all of the frequencies by descending counts. While you are in the "Format" box, also select the "Suppress tables with more than n categories" option and set the maximum number of categories to 100. Most categorical variables have fewer than 100 values. Some of your geographic variables will exceed this amount. You can evaluate those separately if need be. Click to continue and then click the "Statistics" button to add a sum, mean, and other statistics as desired. Click to continue and click "OK".

The output will show the statistics measurements first. You can scroll through to find variables with entirely missing data and observe the statistics to determine whether the file seems correct. Below this statistics box will be frequency tables for all variables with fewer than 100 values.

The charting option is another feature of the frequency distributions dialogue box that many analysts find helpful. This option enables you

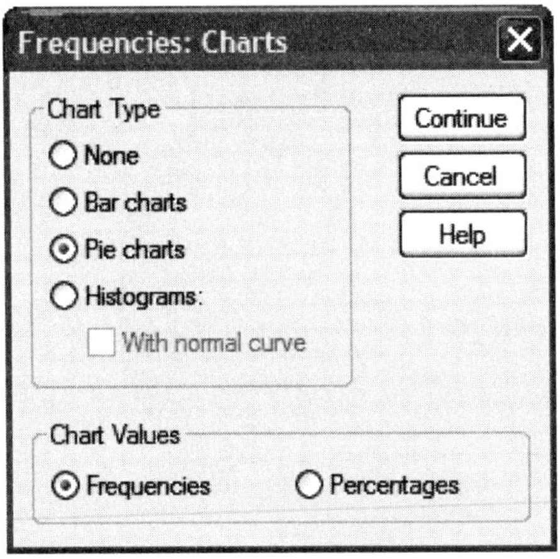

EXHIBIT 8.12   FREQUENCY CHARTS DIALOGUE BOX

to run a quick chart of the results at the same time that you run the frequency distribution calculation. Simply click the chart button and choose the chart type you desire (Exhibit 8.12). If you plan on producing many charts at the same time, I would recommend running frequencies for all of the fields requiring pie charts first. Then, I would run frequencies for all of the fields requiring bar charts, and so on. Also, if you are running several charts at once, I have found it helpful to organize the output by variables using the "Format" dialogue box. This places the frequency distribution (Exhibit 8.13) next to the chart in your output (Exhibit 8.14).

		Frequency	Percent	Valid Percent	Cumulative Percent
Valid	No	36684	73.4	73.4	73.4
	Yes	13316	26.6	26.6	100.0
	Total	50000	100.0	100.0	

EXHIBIT 8.13   FREQUENCY DISTRIBUTION FOR E-MAIL ADDRESS

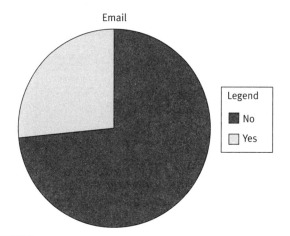

Email

Legend
■ No
☐ Yes

EXHIBIT 8.14	CHART OF FREQUENCY DISTRIBUTION FOR E-MAIL ADDRESS

CROSS TABULATION

The process of comparing the values of two fields is called *cross tabulation*. Some statistics software call this procedure *contingency tables*. For example, if you wanted to know how many event attendees also had e-mail addresses on the database, you would run a cross tabulation between "E-mail" and "Event Attendee". The result could be displayed several ways. You might list just the counts. You might also list the percentage of cases where we know the e-mail address and the individuals also attend events. Or you might list the reverse view of the percentage of event attendees who have e-mail addresses.

To run a cross tabulation in SPSS, select Analyze > Descriptive Statistics > Crosstabs (Exhibit 8.15). Click your e-mail address variable in the row space and your event attendee variable into the column space.

When you click OK, you will see the counts without percentages. To add percentages, click the "Cells" button. Then select "percent of row" or "percent of column". To remember which choice to select, sound it out. "What percent of my row is my column?" or "What percent of my column is my row?" Then replace "row" and "column" with "E-mail" and "Event". To get the answer to "What percent of records with

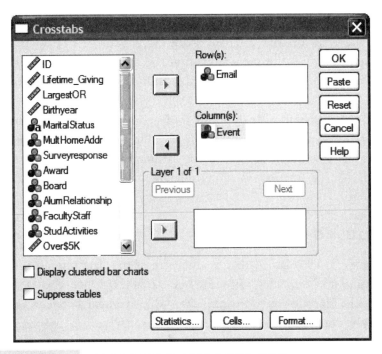

EXHIBIT 8.15   **CROSSTABS DIALOGUE BOX**

e-mail addresses attend events?" use the row checkbox, and vice versa. Exhibit 8.16 is a cross tabulation output showing percent of column.

This cross tabulation shows that 5,989 people have attended events, while 44,011 people have not. Of those who have attended events, 2,558 or 42.7% have e-mail addresses on the database, while 3,431 or 57.3% do

			Event		
			No	Yes	Total
Email	No	Count	33253	3431	36684
		% within Event	75.6%	57.3%	73.4%
	Yes	Count	10758	2558	13316
		% within Event	24.4%	42.7%	26.6%
Total		Count	44011	5989	50000
		% within Event	100.0%	100.0%	100.0%

EXHIBIT 8.16   **CROSS TABULATION OUTPUT**

not. Of those who have not attended events, 10,758 or 24.4% have e-mail addresses on the database while 33,253 or 75.6% do not. The most interesting fact this cross tabulation reveals is the difference between the 24.4% of non-attendees with e-mail addresses and the 42.7% of event attendees with e-mail addresses. Visually, you can see these two fields seem to move together. It does not show you why they move together. This organization might collect e-mail addresses as part of the RSVP process. Perhaps event attendees with e-mail addresses are more easily reached. Maybe there was a considerable event push in the online community.

RECODING VARIABLES

In Chapter 3, I explained that a large part of the data mining process is converting text variables into number variables. Once this is accomplished, the statistics software can observe movement between numbers and apply correlation estimates. Also, the software can use categorical variables as independent characteristics in a model.

There are several ways to change variables in SPSS. You can change the values within a variable, you can create new variables based on the values in existing variables, or you can restructure each value into separate 1/0 variables. There are many other ways to change variables, but these are the most common.

Changing Values of Existing Variables

To change the values within an existing variable, select Transform > Recode into Same Variables (Exhibit 8.17). For this example, let's change the zeros into null values in our lifetime giving field. Select your lifetime giving variable and click the "Old and New Values" button. In this dialogue box, the left side has the old values and the right side holds the new values you intend the old values to become. Type a "0" into the value field in the old value section. Then click the "System Missing" radio button in the new value section, and click "Add". This declares that you want zero to become a null value.

Click continue and then click "OK". Now, all of the zeros have become null values. If you run your descriptive statistics, your valid counts will change to reflect this recode.

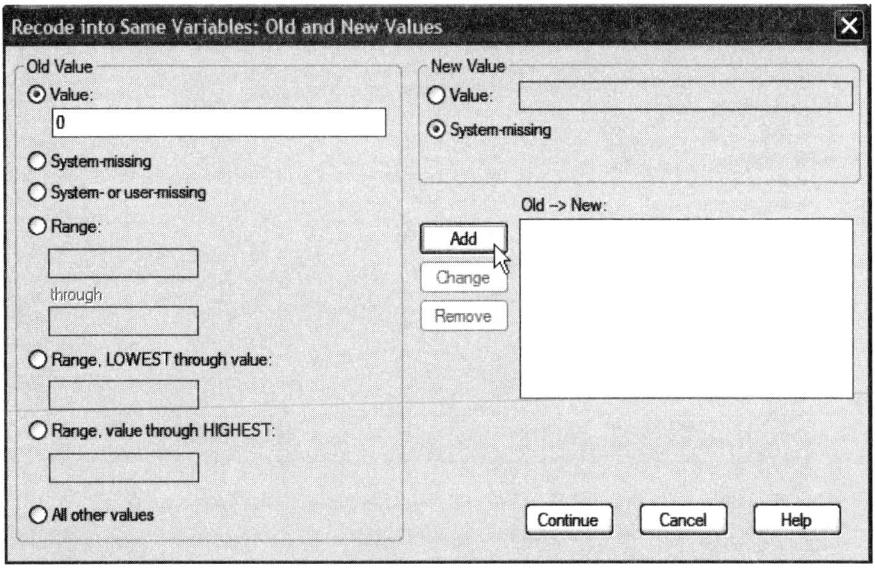

EXHIBIT 8.17   RECODE INTO SAME VARIABLES

Creating New Variables from Old Variables

To create a single yes/no donor field, in which one equals yes and zero equals no, use the same "Recode into Different Variables" dialogue box and select your lifetime giving variable (Exhibit 8.18). Since you are creating a new variable, the dialogue box requires you to provide a name for the new variable. Enter a name in the "Output Variable" space and click "Change". Next, click on the "Old and New Values" button.

This time, select "Range, value through HIGHEST" and type "1". Then type "1" in the new value space and click the "Add" button. This declares that you are changing any case with lifetime giving greater than or equal to "1" into a "1". Next, select "All other values", type "0" in the new value field, and click "Add". This declares that all other valid values less than 1 will be a "0" in the new variable. Then click the "System-or-user-missing" radio button and type "0" into the new value space and click "Add". This declares that null values will also become "0" in the new variable. Click continue and "OK".

You will notice that SPSS has created a new column at the end of your datasheet called "Donor" populated with zeros and ones.

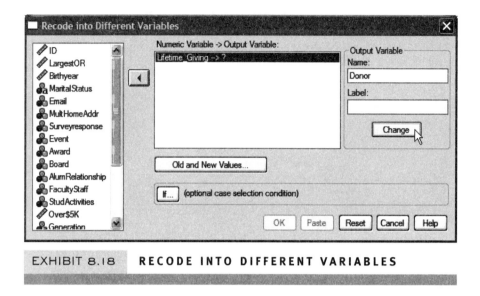

EXHIBIT 8.18   RECODE INTO DIFFERENT VARIABLES

Another way of creating a donor field very quickly is the "Compute" function. To use this, select Transform > Compute Variable (Exhibit 8.19). Enter the name of your new variable into the "Target Variable" space. Then select your lifetime giving variable and move it into the "Numeric Expression" space. Type or click ">=", then type or click "1" and click "OK".

In this case, SPSS creates a new variable at the end of your file where donors are coded with "1" and all the other values are null. After this, you can recode the null values into zeros if need be, using the "Recode into Same Variables" function. If you were using "Donor" as a dependent variable in a model, you would want the nulls to be zeros. If you were using the "Donor" field to analyze characteristics using a custom table, you might want to leave it in the 1/null format. After creating numerous 1/null variables, you can recode all of the nulls into zeros using one "Recode into Same Function". If you plan to recode numerous variables, this might be a more efficient approach than using the "Recode into Different Variables" function.

Restructuring Variables

Let's say we wanted to create a unique 1/0 variable for each value in the marital status field. We could use the "Recode into Different Variables"

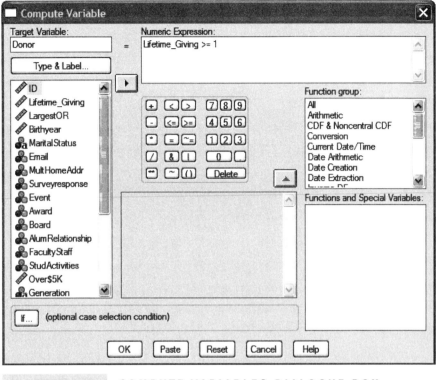

EXHIBIT 8.19   **COMPUTE VARIABLES DIALOGUE BOX**

function, type "Married" into the old values space with a "1" in the new values space, and assign zeros to all other values and null cases. Then we would need to repeat the process for each of the other values. If we had a very large categorical variable, such as "State", it would take a great deal of time to finish all of the recodes. A simpler approach is restructuring the data.

Restructuring can automatically assign a new 1/0 variable to every value in a field. To restructure in SPSS, select Data > Restructure. It will prompt you to save the file. I recommend doing this so you can revert in case you make an error in the restructuring process. Select the "Restructure selected cases into variables" radio button and click "Next" (Exhibit 8.20).

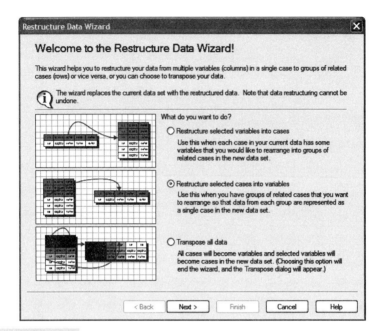

EXHIBIT 8.20   **RESTRUCTURE DATA WIZARD**

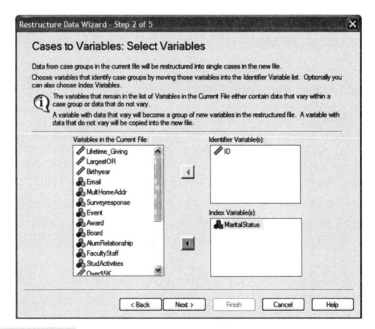

EXHIBIT 8.21   **RESTRUCTURE DATA WIZARD: SELECT VARIABLES**

Move your unique ID into the "Identifier Variable(s)" space, move your marital status field into the "Index Variable(s)" space, and click "Next" (Exhibit 8.21).

SPSS will ask you about sorting the data. This is fine to do. Go ahead and select the "Yes" radio button and click "Next". On the next dialogue box, check the "Indicator Variables" checkbox and type a root name for your new variables. Click "Next" and then "Finish" to run the restructure process (Exhibit 8.22).

Now you will have a new column for each value in your marital status column. If your values contained spaces or started with numbers, SPSS will assign a new name to the variable. If your marital status field had some cases with only spaces and no text, SPSS will not restructure until you recode those spaces into text. If it changed names, it will indicate this in the output and assign labels for those variables. Exhibit 8.23 shows an example.

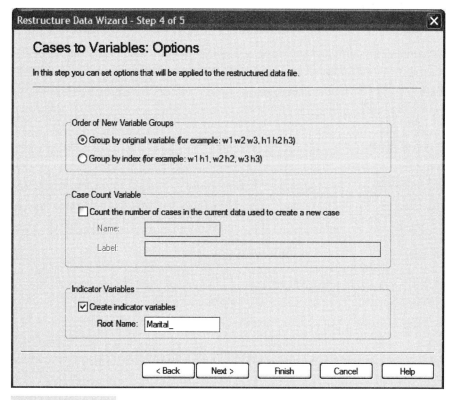

EXHIBIT 8.22   RESTRUCTURE DATA WIZARD: OPTIONS

Original Variable	MaritalStatus	Result	
		Name	Label
Indicator	Divorced	Marital_Divorced	
	Domestic Partne	ind1	Marital_Domestic Partne
	Formerly marrie	ind2	Marital_Formerly marrie
	Married	Marital_Married	
	Separated	Marital_Separated	
	Single	Marital_Single	
	Unknown Marital	ind3	Marital_Unknown Marital
	Widowed	Marital_Widowed	

EXHIBIT 8.23   RESTRUCTURED VARIABLES OUTPUT WITH LABELS FOR INVALID FIELD NAMES

CORRELATION

I explained in Chapter 3 that correlation is a technique used to see if variables move together. We saw a visual relationship between attending an event and having an e-mail address in the section on cross tabulation. In SPSS, you can measure whether two numeric variables are correlated using the cross tabulation function.

Let's say we wanted to measure the correlation between attending an event and giving a gift. We would start by producing a cross tabulation. Select Analyze > Descriptive Statistics > Crosstabs. Move your event field into the row space and the donor field into the column space. Click the "Statistics" button, check the "Correlations" checkbox, and click to continue. Click the "Cells" button, and select the column percentage. Then click to continue and click "OK" (Exhibit 8.24).

First, you will see the cross tabulation. As you compare the percentage of non-donors with event attendance to the percentage of donors with event attendance, you may see there is a significant difference (Exhibit 8.25).

Next you will see the measurements of correlation. The Pearson's R is used for comparing variables of this type. If you are comparing ordinal variables, such as rankings, you would use the Spearman Correlation. These values range from -1 to 1. If every donor also was an event attendee and every non-donor was not an event attendee, the Pearson's R would be 1. If every donor was not an event attendee and every non-donor was an

			Donor		
			.00	1.00	Total
Event	0	Count	26065	17946	44011
		% within Donor	91.9%	82.9%	88.0%
	1	Count	2294	3695	5989
		% within Donor	8.1%	17.1%	12.0%
Total		Count	28359	21641	50000
		% within Donor	100.0%	100.0%	100.0%

EXHIBIT 8.24   CROSS TABULATION OF EVENT AND DONOR WITH NUMERIC FIELD VALUES

event attendee, the Pearson's R would be −1. If the Pearson's R value was 0, there would be no correlation. The further the value is from 0, the stronger the correlation whether a positive or negative value.

Most analysts would first look at the "Approximate Significance" of this output first. If this value is less than 0.01, the measurement is significant in more than 99% of the population. If the value is less than 0.05, the measurement is significant in more than 95% of the population. If the value is greater than 0.05, the significance is too low to pay much attention to the correlation, and most analysts discard it.

I often pay the most attention to correlation values above 0.1 (absolute value) with acceptable significance. These are the strongest correlations. Correlation values above 0.05 (absolute value) are still noteworthy. And mild correlations of 0.025 (absolute value) may catch my attention in some analyses.

If you wanted to find the correlation of several variables to being a donor, you might use the "Correlations" function on SPSS. Select Analyze > Correlate > Bivariate (Exhibit 8.26). Move the donor

		Value	Asymp. Std. Error[a]	Approx. T[b]	Approx. Sig.
Interval by Interval	Pearson's R	.137	.004	30.948	.000[c]
Ordinal by Ordinal	Spearman Correlation	.137	.004	30.948	.000[c]
N of Valid Cases		50000			

a. Not assuming the null hypothesis.

b. Using the asymptotic standard error assuming the null hypothesis.

c. Based on normal approximation.

EXHIBIT 8.25   CORRELATION STATISTICS OUTPUT

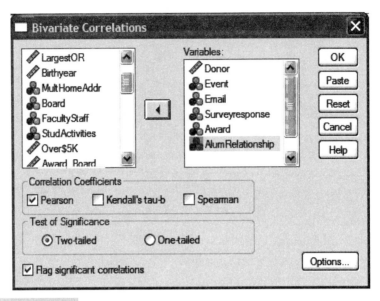

EXHIBIT 8.26 BIVARIATE CORRELATIONS DIALOGUE BOX

		Donor	Event	Email	Surveyre sponse	Award	Alum Relationship
Donor	Pearson Correlation	1	.137**	.078**	-.189**	-.032**	.112**
	Sig. (2-tailed)		.000	.000	.000	.000	.000
	N	50000	50000	50000	50000	50000	50000
Event	Pearson Correlation	.137**	1	.134**	.033**	.069**	.142**
	Sig. (2-tailed)	.000		.000	.000	.000	.000
	N	50000	50000	50000	50000	50000	50000
Email	Pearson Correlation	.078**	.134**	1	.155**	.049**	.126**
	Sig. (2-tailed)	.000	.000		.000	.000	.000
	N	50000	50000	50000	50000	50000	50000
Surveyresponse	Pearson Correlation	-.189**	.033**	.155**	1	.033**	.184**
	Sig. (2-tailed)	.000	.000	.000		.000	.000
	N	50000	50000	50000	50000	50000	50000
Award	Pearson Correlation	-.032**	.069**	.049**	.033**	1	.046**
	Sig. (2-tailed)	.000	.000	.000	.000		.000
	N	50000	50000	50000	50000	50000	50000
AlumRelationship	Pearson Correlation	.112**	.142**	.126**	.184**	.046**	1
	Sig. (2-tailed)	.000	.000	.000	.000	.000	
	N	50000	50000	50000	50000	50000	50000

**. Correlation is significant at the 0.01 level (2-tailed).

EXHIBIT 8.27 BIVARIATE CORRELATION OUTPUT

field into the variables space, followed by the other binary (1/0) variables you wish to analyze. Select the "Pearson" checkbox and click "OK".

SPSS will produce a grid showing the relationship between all of these variables. You can right-click on this grid and paste it into spreadsheet software such as Excel to sort it. All of the information you need to know is in the first column of data. This shows the relationship of each variable to the donor variable (Exhibit 8.27).

The significance of all of these variables is below 0.05, so they are all worth consideration. The most correlated variable to giving among these five variables is an inverse relationship. Survey response appears to move in the opposite direction of giving in this file.

CORRELATION RANKING

A popular technique for building a quick score is to add the most correlated factors together. To do this, you first run your correlation calculations to determine which five to ten variables have the strongest relationships. Next, recode your inverse relationships, using the "Recode into Different Variables" to make "Did not respond to survey" or "Did not receive an award". Basically, "1" becomes "0" and "0" becomes "1". Then you add the variables together.

To add the variables in SPSS, select Transform > Compute Variable. Next, name your new correlation score. Then move each variable into the "Numeric Expression" space and type or click "+" in between them. After you click "OK", SPSS will create a new score variable at the end of your datasheet (Exhibit 8.28).

Now, run a cross tabulation between the correlation score and donor variable. This time, select the percentage of the correlation score and select the correlation checkbox. First, let's look at the cross tabulation (Exhibit 8.29).

As the score increases, the percentage of donors increases by group. Of the 200 people matching all five characteristics, only four are not donors. Of the 1,605 people who have four of the characteristics, 1,319 or 82.2% are also donors.

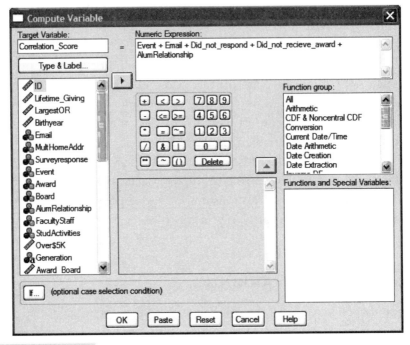

EXHIBIT 8.28 **COMPUTING A CORRELATION RANKING SCORE**

			Donor		
			.00	1.00	Total
Correlation_Score	.00	Count	389	120	509
		% within Correlation_Score	76.4%	23.6%	100.0%
	1.00	Count	10769	3673	14442
		% within Correlation_Score	74.6%	25.4%	100.0%
	2.00	Count	13641	12121	25762
		% within Correlation_Score	53.0%	47.0%	100.0%
	3.00	Count	3270	4212	7482
		% within Correlation_Score	43.7%	56.3%	100.0%
	4.00	Count	286	1319	1605
		% within Correlation_Score	17.8%	82.2%	100.0%
	5.00	Count	4	196	200
		% within Correlation_Score	2.0%	98.0%	100.0%
Total		Count	28359	21641	50000
		% within Correlation_Score	56.7%	43.3%	100.0%

EXHIBIT 8.29 **CROSS TABULATION OF CORRELATION RANKING SCORE AND DONOR**

	Value	Asymp. Std. Error[a]	Approx. T[b]	Approx. Sig.
Interval by Interval Pearson's R	.270	.004	62.600	.000[c]
Ordinal by Ordinal Spearman Correlation	.264	.004	61.278	.000[c]
N of Valid Cases	50000			

a. Not assuming the null hypothesis.

b. Using the asymptotic standard error assuming the null hypothesis.

c. Based on normal approximation.

EXHIBIT 8.30   **CORRELATIONS STATISTICS FOR CROSS TABULATION OF CORRELATION RANKING SCORE AND DONOR**

Now let's look at the Pearson's R (Exhibit 8.30). The relationship in this combined score is greater than any of the variables by themselves. In prospecting, you might build a score like this measuring correlations to major giving. You would start by looking at the fives that are not major donors, then the fours, and so on. It is likely that you will find people who fit the profile of your major donors, but are not yet major donors.

I have found some challenges with this approach, too. At the top of the score, you frequently see a tremendous decrease in your counts. I get to the lower score levels too soon in implementation. Also, if I am trying to slice and dice a mail file, I do not have enough flexibility to move my cut points. More often than not, I use this process to make new variables I might use later in a regression formula.

CALCULATING DATABASE CAPACITY

In Chapter 4, I described the process of calculating a combined capacity score. If you have a data file containing all of your wealth data and existing ratings, this is relatively easy to accomplish. The process includes four primary steps:

Step 1. Prepare your data for consolidation
Step 2. Combine the data using a compute function
Step 3. Verify your results
Step 4. Recode into ranges

Prepare Your Data for Consolidation

The first step of the process is to take all of your wealth data that is not already in a numeric format and convert it. Many organizations maintain capacity amounts in text ranges such as "$1 million to $2 million" or "$25,000 to $50,000". For these variables, use the recode function as described above to make them a single dollar amount.

If you are trying to decide which value to select from a range, you are safest using the bottom value. I have used the median value if the ranges are tight. It is better to be conservative in this analysis.

Combine the Data Using a Compute Function

In Chapter 4, I presented the following formula for calculating capacity:

- Existing capacity rating from the prospect research department
- Existing capacity ratings from screening
- 25% of insider stock holdings (direct holdings and vested options)
- 10% of equity in private companies
- 1% of private company sales, if the individual is a top executive
- 5% of real estate totaling less than $1 million
- 10% of real estate totaling between $1 million and $1.9 million
- 20% of real estate totaling more than $2 million
- 10% of all other identified assets such as art, aircraft, boats, external wealth scores
- 10% of identified income
- 10% of a published net worth amount
- Five times the largest cash gift total in a single fiscal year
- 5% of median income by ZIP code
- 5% of median value of owner occupied housing by ZIP code

Select Transform > Compute Variable. Create a capacity estimate based on each distinct metric. Using Net Worth as an example, create a target variable called "Capacity from Net Worth". Move your net worth variable into the "Numeric Expression" space. Type or click "*" followed by "0.1" and click "OK". This will create a new variable at the end of your datasheet, indicating the capacity estimate derived only from net worth (Exhibit 8.31).

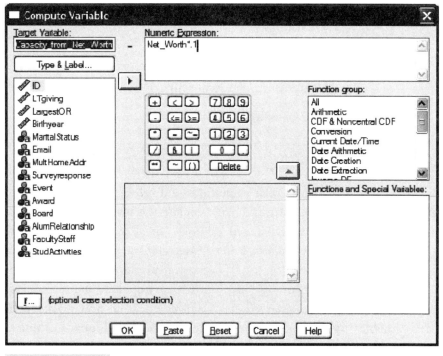

EXHIBIT 8.31   **COMPUTING A CAPACITY ESTIMATE FROM A SINGLE WEALTH INDICATOR**

Repeat this process for each variable where the capacity is a percentage or a multiple of the dollar amount. You will end up with the following derived variables:

- Capacity from stockholdings*
- Capacity from private company equity
- Capacity from private company sales
- Capacity from real estate under $1 million
- Capacity from real estate, $1 to $2 million
- Capacity from real estate over $2 million
- Capacity from other assets

---

*In SPSS you will need to replace the spaces with underscores (_).

- Capacity from income
- Capacity from net worth
- Capacity from largest cash gift
- Capacity from median income
- Capacity from median home ownership

The following variables will not change:

- Existing capacity rating from the prospect research department
- Existing capacity ratings from screening

Next, recode any zero dollar values into null values using the "Recode into Same Variables" function. Then calculate the maximum from all of these capacities and the unchanged variables. In SPSS, open the "Compute Variables" dialogue again. Enter "Overall_Capacity" as your target variable. Then, using the "Statistical" option from the "Function" group, find and double-click on "Max". This will populate the "Numeric Expression" box with "MAX(?,?)". Replace the question marks with your variables by highlighting a question mark and double-clicking a capacity variable. Keep populating the expression until all of the variables are between the parentheses, with commas separating them. You can also type the expression directly into the "Numeric Expression" box. Click "OK" (Exhibit 8.32).

SPSS will create a new variable by selecting the highest value from all of the capacity estimates. You might also follow the same process to determine the mean of the capacity estimates.

Using the compute dialogue box, you can also combine these steps. Exhibit 8.33 demonstrates this possibility.

Verify Your Results

The outcome of this composite capacity formula is one capacity amount for each constituent, when data is present. It is important to hand-verify the very top capacity amounts. I also randomly spot-check several other levels of the other capacities to determine whether there were any problems with the calculations. If my goal is to use this list to identify possible wealthy suspects we might have overlooked, I might forward the top unmanaged names directly to prospect research for qualification. If my goal is to assess the potential of the overall fundraising database,

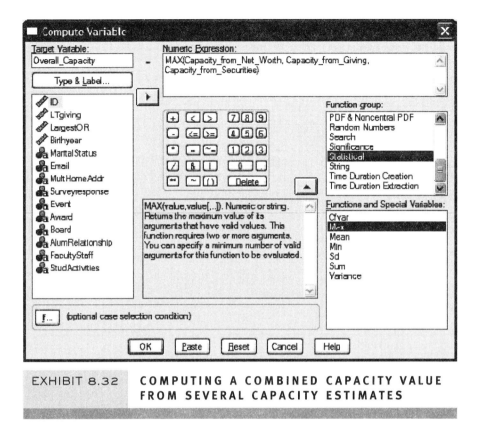

EXHIBIT 8.32   **COMPUTING A COMBINED CAPACITY VALUE FROM SEVERAL CAPACITY ESTIMATES**

I might smooth all of the values above the top level of the pyramid to the bottom number of this pyramid range. If I were to make any changes, I would create a new variable first so I would not change my original data.

If there are substantial levels of missing value, your might choose to fill them using the "Replace Missing Values" function in SPSS. I would sort the file by ZIP+4 or age and assign the average value or the median value of the five or so records on either side of the missing value. Select Transform > Replace Missing Values. Move your capacity value or one of the capacity indicators into the "New Variable(s)" space, select your method of replacing values, the span of nearby points, and click the "Change" button. Click "OK". SPSS will create a new variable with the missing values filled in. This new variable might be incorporated into your formula to enhance your composite capacity score (Exhibit 8.34).

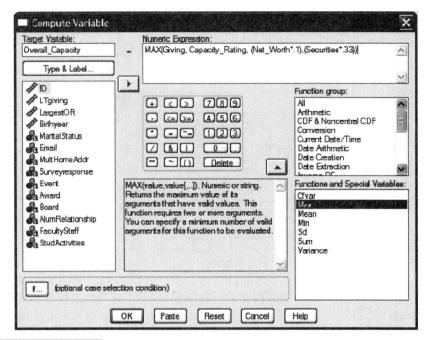

EXHIBIT 8.33   **COMPUTING THE INDIVIDUAL CAPACITY ESTIMATES AND OVERALL VALUE IN ONE STEP**

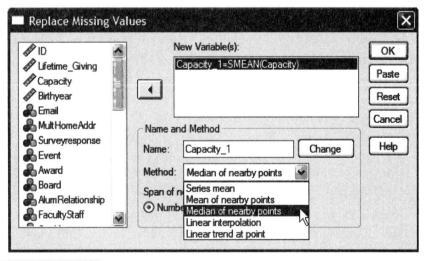

EXHIBIT 8.34   **REPLACE MISSING VALUES DIALOGUE BOX**

Recode into Ranges

When I have finished creating my capacity score, I find it helpful to recode the score to match the gift levels of the campaign planning pyramid. To do this, simply use the "Recode into Different Variables" function. I will demonstrate this using a sample file and abbreviated ranges. Select Transform > Recode into Different Variables, and move your new capacity field into the "Numeric Variable → Output Variable" space. Type a new name for your range field, click "Change", and then select "Old and New Values".

For this recode function, you are changing a numeric variable to a string variable. SPSS will always assume you are creating numeric variables unless you tell it otherwise. Check the "Output variables are strings" checkbox and make the width large enough to accommodate your pyramid ranges (Exhibit 8.35).

Next, use the "Range" options to type in the dollar ranges of your gift pyramid. In the "New Value" spaces, use a descriptive label and click "Add" for each level. I like to use a letter or number before the range so

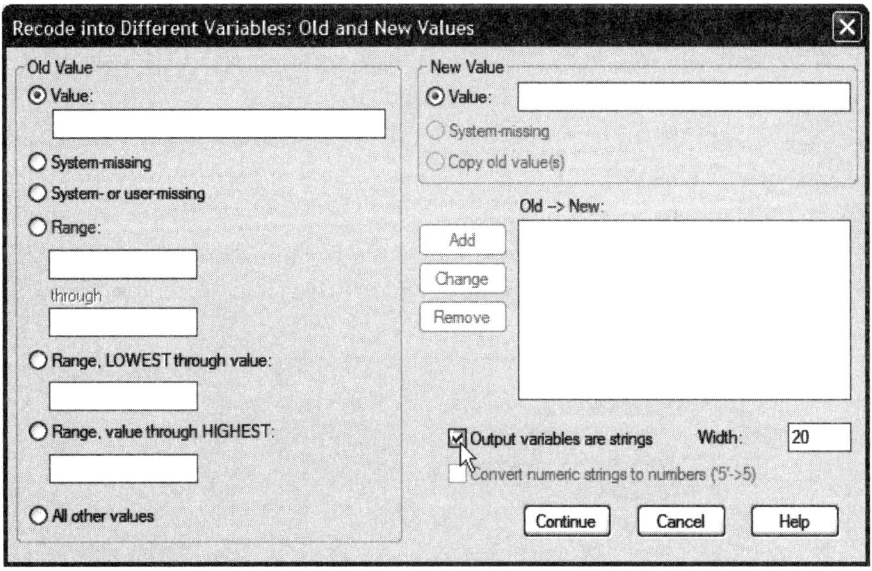

EXHIBIT 8.35   CHECKING THE STRING OPTION WHEN RECODING INTO DIFFERENT VARIABLES

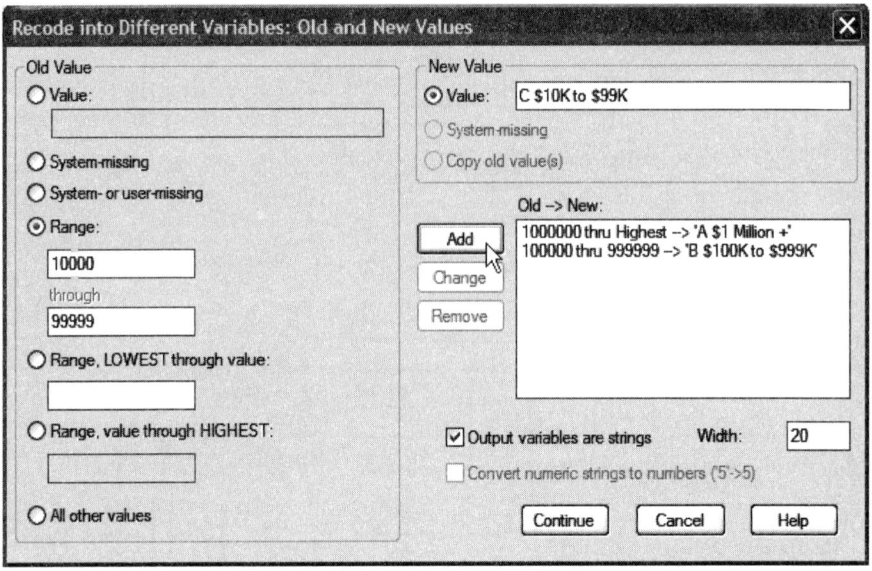

EXHIBIT 8.36   RECODING DOLLAR LEVELS INTO RANGES

that future charts and operations will default to my intended order. When you are finished, click to continue and click "OK" (Exhibit 8.36).

SPSS will create a new string field at the end of your data sheet. To verify the values of your new range field, run a frequency distribution. It will show you the distribution by each level and also reveal whether you missed any values in your recode. Exhibit 8.37 shows a frequency table based on the abbreviated sample.

In most actual files, I will group all variables less than $10,000 together as the bottom level of my range, since most gift pyramids begin at

		Frequency	Percent	Valid Percent	Cumulative Percent
Valid	A $1 Million +	10	.0	.0	.0
	B $100K to $999K	28	.1	.1	.1
	C $10K to $99K	206	.4	.4	.5
	D $1K to $9K	1682	3.4	3.4	3.9
	E < $1K	48074	96.1	96.1	100.0
	Total	50000	100.0	100.0	

EXHIBIT 8.37   FREQUENCY DISTRIBUTION OF DOLLAR RANGES

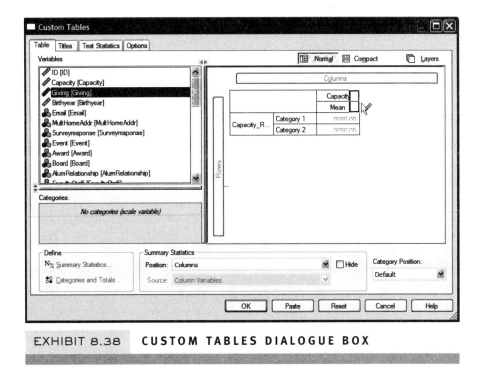

$10,000. After you calculate these ranges, you may wish to see the average actual capacity for each of the ranges, as well as the average and total gifts. I prefer to use the custom tables function from the Tables module, which does not come in the SPSS base product. To do this in SPSS, select Analyze > Tables > Custom Tables. Click and drag the capacity ranges field onto the "Row" bar on the left side of the design space. Then click and drag the capacity dollar field into the "Column" bar on the top of the design space. Then click and drag your giving or five-year giving total to the right of the capacity field (Exhibit 8.38).

Next, click the "Summary Statistics" option to select mean, median, and sum. If the "Summary Statistics" option is grayed out, simply click on one of the column variables. Select "Apply to All" and click "OK" (Exhibit 8.39).

SPSS will create the table shown in Exhibit 8.40 as your output.

This same process of recoding your capacity fields might be used on your target ask amounts and giving fields, as well. Using the "Custom Tables" function makes it very easy to include all of those values and overlay prospects and suspects to fill your gift pyramid.

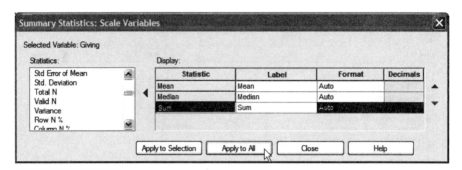

EXHIBIT 8.39   SUMMARY STATISTICS OPTIONS FOR CUSTOM TABLES

		Capacity			Giving		
		Mean	Median	Sum	Mean	Median	Sum
Capacity_Ranges	A $1 Million +	$2,517,366	$1,605,355	$25,173,662	$1,014,784	$843,839	$10,147,836
	B $100K to $999K	$252,066	$186,073	$7,057,838	$141,826	$97,500	$3,971,137
	C $10K to $99K	$26,249	$18,743	$5,407,303	$10,679	$5,114	$2,199,919
	D $1K to $9K	$2,487	$1,850	$4,183,907	$618	$278	$1,039,493
	E < $1K	$153	$73	$3,026,230	$55	$35	$1,250,604

EXHIBIT 8.40   CUSTOM TABLE OUTPUT DISPLAYING GIVING PYRAMID DATA

RFM ANALYSIS

In Chapter 6, I presented a formula for calculating a basic snapshot of recency, frequency, and monetary value (RFM) to measure constituent value. This formula is relatively easy to produce using the SPSS techniques we have already covered. Below are the three primary pieces with basic instructions for producing the score.

Recency, *max score = 20*	
Gave in last year	20
Gave 1–2 years ago	15
Gave 2–3 years ago	10
Gave 3–4 years ago	5
Gave 4–5 years ago	2
Gave more than 5 years ago	1
No giving	0

If you have actual dates and not fiscal years for your gift dates, you can use the "Date and Time Wizard" under "Transform" to extract years or calculate them using the date fields. If you have fiscal years, simply open your compute variables function. Subtract the year of the most recent gift from the current fiscal year to determine the number of years since the last gift. Then recode these numbers into the point values and call that new variable "Recency".

Frequency, *max score = 30*

Frequency% Score	
(Gift Count) / [(Last gift year) − (First gift year)]	
100%	10 (to be multiplied by years-giving multiplier)
90–99%	8
80–89%	6
70–79%	4
60–69%	2
<60%	1
Years-giving multiplier	
20+ years giving	(Frequency % score) * 3.0 = Frequency
15–19 years giving	(Frequency % score) * 2.5 = Frequency
10–14 years giving	(Frequency % score) * 2.0 = Frequency
5–9 years giving	(Frequency % score) * 1.5 = Frequency
<5 years giving	(Frequency % score) * 1 = Frequency
No giving	0 = Frequency score

To calculate your frequency statistics, you will need to take a few more steps. First, subtract the first gift year from the most recent gift year to determine the number of years giving. Recode these values into a different variable called, "Years giving multiplier"* and wait with that for a moment. Now, divide the total gift count by the years giving and call this variable "Frequency percent". Recode "Frequency percent" into the scores and call the new variable "Frequency percent score", or something similar. Then, use the compute function to multiply the "Frequency

---

*Remember to use underscores (_) in place of spaces for column headings.

percent score" by the "Years giving multiplier" and name this new variable "Frequency".

Monetary Value, *max score = 50 (Set gift amounts that make sense for your organization)*

$5,000+ outright gift	25
$2,000−$4,999 outright gift	15
$1,000−$1,999 outright gift	10
$500−$999 outright gift	5
<$500	1
No giving	0
$20,000+ cumulative giving	Additional 25
$10,000−$19,999	Additional 15
$5,000−$9,999	Additional 5
RFM Score, max score = 100	
Sum of Recency, Frequency, and Monetary Value Scores	

Recode your largest outright gift amount into the scores shown above and name that variable "Monetary Value Outright." Next, recode your lifetime giving variable into the scores shown above, with all totals below $5,000 recoded to "0." Name this variable "Monetary Value Cumulative". Then add "Monetary Value Outright" and "Monetary Value Cumulative" together, using the compute function. This new variable should be named "Monetary Value". Finally, add "Recency", "Frequency", and "Monetary Value" together, and name that variable "RFM Score".

ATTACHMENT SCORE

In Chapter 4, I described incorporating attachment or connection scores into your campaign planning to determine how close constituents are to your organization. Building this score is possible using the techniques already covered. Here are the steps to producing the weighted health care attachment score. The formula is as follows:

Step 1. Patient: 5 points
Step 2. Patient family: 5 points

Step 3. Donor: 5 points

Step 4. Gift count:
- 10 or more gifts: 10 points
- 5 to 9 gifts: 5 points

Step 5. Manager: 20 points

Step 6. Any board, support group, or group membership: 5 points per board/group

Step 7. Total contacts × 3 = points

Step 8. Current campaign prospect: 30 points

Step 9. Years since last gift
- Lowest through 2: 10 points
- . . . through 5: 5 points
- . . . through 10: 2 points

In SPSS, recode your patient field so that "yes" or "1" becomes "5", and your null fields and existing "0"s are all "0". You might recode into the same variables unless you will use this same data file for other purposes. If so, name the new variable "Patient Score". Follow the same process for family members of patients, donors, managed constituents, boards, support groups, memberships, and prospects.

For your gift count, recode into a different variable, using the "Range" options to assign the points listed above. If a constituent has fewer than five gifts, recode them as "0". For the years since last gift, similar to RFM, subtract the most recent gift date from the current gift date, using either the compute function for year values or the Date and Time Wizard for full date fields.

After you have the points produced for each of these variables, add them together using the compute function and name this variable "Attachment". If there are null values in your attachment score, go back and recode all of your point variables to be sure that null values are "0". Then add the variables together again.

This approach gives you a quick snapshot of attachment. If you ran it periodically, you would see scores increase as individuals increased their participation. If you wanted to model the likelihood of becoming attached, you might build a regression model with this attachment score as the dependent variable.

CHAPTER 9

Regression Analysis

O ne of the most effective ways to identify new prospects or segment a file for annual giving is through predictive modeling. Of the many varieties of models, including decision trees, clusters, and neural networks, the most prevalent approach is regression analysis. As with all analysis projects, remember to plan your regression analysis by using the CRISP-DM process outlined throughout the book. Again, those stages are:

- *Business Understanding:* Defining the context of the analysis
- *Data Understanding:* Aligning data elements to the context
- *Data Preparation:* Gathering and priming the data for analysis
- *Modeling:* Conducting the analysis
- *Evaluation:* Determining if the analysis supports the goal of the business understanding
- *Deployment:* Implementing the analysis

DEFINE BUSINESS NEED OR GOAL

Start by asking yourself, "What are we trying to predict?" How will you use this model when it is finished? Some of the most common models fundraising analytics professionals construct are the following:

- Major giving prospect identification
- Planned giving prospect identification
- Overall giving likelihood, to prioritize never-donor appeals
- Likelihood to increase participation or become engaged in alumni association
- Affinity toward the institution
- Predicting donors most likely to renew and upgrade a gift

- Identification of future volunteers and board members
- Channel response likelihood

DETERMINE REQUIRED DATA ELEMENTS

Whichever model you choose, you need to define the dependent variable. This is the existing behavior you are setting out to model. Then you need to define your independent variables. These are all the characteristics that are independent of the behavior, meaning they do not exist because the behavior exists. For example, if your only means of acquiring e-mail addresses is from donor reply cards, you would not use e-mail addresses to predict giving. It is not independent of giving.

In a fundraising database, there is much debate about how independent much of the data actually is. Since it is a relationship management system, constituents with stronger relationships will have more information. One could argue that most of the data in the system exists because giving behavior exists. It might not exist because a specific type of giving behavior exists, but there is some relationship nonetheless. The only way to have the variables be purely independent is to use completely external data.

There are simple reasons why analysts are cautious about using data that exists because major giving behavior exists. The model will produce people already on the radar. At the same time, I suspect if you built a model fully using this endogenous data, your model would still have constituents with high scorers that are unknown to an organization. If your model is to be truly predictive, you need to control for this internal bias. However, if your goal is to identify prospects and pass them on to prospecting identification specialists who will qualify your results, you have some flexibility. I prefer to draw the line between data that exists because of the behavior and data that might exist partially because of the data. The line that divides the data you use from the data you don't use will be different depending on the project. You will develop an instinct for which data elements to use over time.

For most of the independent variables, I start with a very big file. I do not try to imagine which characteristics might predict the behavior. Instead, I start with just about every characteristic I can extract, except extremely endogenous elements. I met with a Kansas City artist named

David Logan who also works in nonprofit fundraising. He used an analogy that has always stuck with me for assembling a data file. He described how artists will plan the colors for a painting based on the primary colors. Roughly two-thirds of a painting would be based in one of the primary colors. Of the other third, two-thirds of that will be based on another primary color. Then, the final ninth will be based on the remaining primary color. That final ninth is the subject of the painting. If you want the red of the roses to jump out, eight-ninths of the painting will be in blue- and yellow-based tones. If you want your major donors to jump out, it is important to have lots of blue and yellow paint in your data file.

The dependent variables should match the behavior you hope to predict as exactly as possible. Here are dependent variables I would use for the common models I listed.

Model	Dependent variable
Major giving prospect identification	Major Donors • Existing major donors = 1 • All other records = 0
Planned giving prospect identification	Planned Gift Donors • Existing planned gift donors = 1 • All other records = 0
Overall giving likelihood to prioritize never donor appeals	Donors • All donors excluding tribute-only or dues = 1, may also use recent donors only • All other records = 0
Likelihood to increase participation or become engaged in alumni association	Attachment score • The actual linear score from a point system
Affinity toward the institution	High Affinity constituents • Constituents with survey responses indicating high affinity = 1 • All other records = 0
Predicting donors most likely to renew and upgrade a gift	Consecutive upgrades • Donors with consecutive increasing gifts = 1 • All other records = 0

(Continued)

| Identification of future volunteers and board members | Volunteers
Current or former board members = 1
All other records = 0 |
| Channel response likelihood | Top producing channel
Highest total giving from mail = 1
Highest total giving from phone = 2
Highest total giving online = 3
Highest total giving in person or other = 4
Non-donors and ties = 0 |

MODEL SELECTION

As your analytics program grows, you will learn a great variety of models. The varieties of models are vast and varied. Most of them depend on the nature of the variables in your model. Your variables will be either nominal, ordinal, or scale.

Nominal

Also called categorical or logistic, nominal variable values represent categories with no intrinsic ranking; for example, the department of the company in which an employee works. Examples of nominal variables include yes/no variables, channels, volunteers, gender, marital status, region, ZIP code, and religious affiliation.

Ordinal

The values of ordinal variables represent categories with some intrinsic ranking; for example, levels of service satisfaction, from highly dissatisfied to highly satisfied. Examples of ordinal variables include attitude scores representing degree of satisfaction or confidence, preference ranking scores, "A, B, C" propensity rankings, and gift levels.

Scale

A variable can be treated as a scale when its values are represented linearly, so that distance comparisons between values are appropriate. Examples of scale variables include total giving dollars, attachment scores, RFM scores, age in years, and capacity in dollars.

When analysts have binary nominal variables (1/0) as their dependent, they might choose to use decision trees or binary logistic regression. If they have many nominal categories in their dependent variable, they might use multinomial logistic regression or discriminant analysis. If analysts are trying to predict a ranking or a gift level, they might use ordinal regression. When they predict giving or large numeric scores, they would use linear regression. If they do not know the groupings for a dependent and want the software to discover it, they would use cluster analysis. Again, there are many other varieties I have not listed. Many different types of models will become facile to advanced analysts.

To demonstrate the principles of modeling, I will use a relatively simple type of regression analysis called *binary logistic regression*. To illustrate the process, I will use the same sample data file used in Chapter 8 to show the correlation ranking score.

PREPARE THE DATA FOR MODELING

Begin by creating numeric variables using the process covered in Chapter 8. First, create your "donor" variable by recoding constituents with non-tribute and non-dues lifetime giving greater than $0 with a "1". Then recode all others and null values to "0." Follow this same process to create nominal and ordinal variables for all of your independent characteristics.

For scores and other scale variables, create rankings in groups of three, five, or ten, depending on the variable. In a major giving model, I might incorporate a ranking of first gift amount, recency, frequency, or springboard effects (current gift amount compared to previous averages, sometimes called "velocity" by analysts). To do this in SPSS, select Transform > Rank Cases, move your scale variable into the "Variable(s)" space, and click "Rank Types". Uncheck the "Rank" checkbox and check the "Ntiles" checkbox. Type in your number of groups, click to continue, and click "OK". SPSS will create a new ordinal variable at the end of your datasheet (Exhibit 9.1).

After you create all of your 1/0 and ordinal variables, make sure there are no null values. You can run frequency distributions to uncover missing values. For most variables indicating presence of data, null is equal to zero. Use Recode into Same Function to make this change. For some

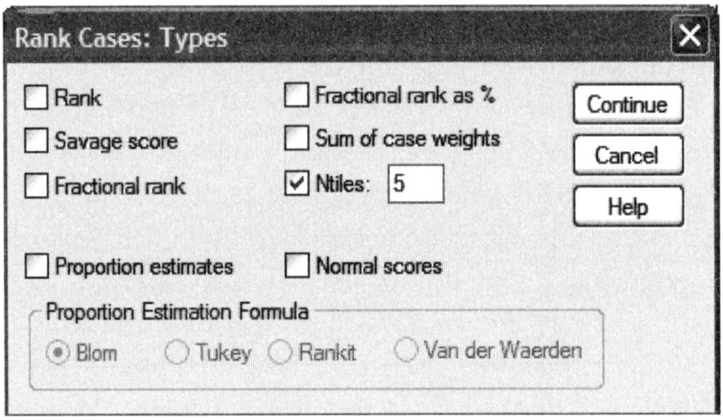

EXHIBIT 9.1   RANK CASES: TYPES DIALOGUE BOX

ordinals, the mean or the median is the true neutral value. A survey response of affinity might be: 5 = high affinity, 4 = affinity, 3 = neutral, 2 = dislikes, 1 = strongly dislikes. If a constituent did not fill out the survey, the feeling is unknown, and the field value is null. If you leave null values in your model, you will exclude the case. I would code nonresponses as "3" instead of "0" if I were to use the variable. In the ranking, "0" would be treated as worse than "strongly dislikes".

Selection Sample

I have found it effective to have an equal number of ones and zeros when I build binary logistic regression models. That way, when I evaluate my model, a 50% cut value will be more informative. I describe the cut value later, in the model evaluation section. You would construct this sample or series of samples in the data preparation stages.

For major giving models, I like to have a sample made up of half major donors and the other half randomly selected. Since the major giving pool is small, I will create several samples to model and compare. For an overall giving model like this one, a single sample is generally sufficient.

To create this sample, first sort your file ascending by the dependent variable. In SPSS, simply right-click on the column heading and select "Sort Ascending". Then run a frequency distribution on your dependent variable (Exhibit 9.2).

		Frequency	Percent	Valid Percent	Cumulative Percent
Valid	.00	28359	56.7	56.7	56.7
	1.00	21641	43.3	43.3	100.0
	Total	50000	100.0	100.0	

EXHIBIT 9.2   **FREQUENCY DISTRIBUTION FOR DEPENDENT VARIABLE**

In this file of 50,000 records, less than half are donors (21,641). I want to have an equal pool of donors and non-donors, so I need 21,641 randomly selected non-donors.

Now that you know the counts for your sample and your file is sorted ascending, select Data > Select Cases. Be sure the "Filter out unselected cases" radio button is selected. Next, click the "Random sample of cases" radio button (Exhibit 9.3).

Next, click the radio button next to the word "Exactly", and fill it in to read "Exactly 21,641 from the first 28,359 cases" or whatever your numbers from the frequency distribution happen to be. Click to continue and click "OK" (Exhibit 9.4).

Your selection will be selected, and SPSS will add a filter variable to the end of the datasheet. This variable was the goal of the selection, so now we should reselect all the cases. Go back into the Select Cases dialogue and select "All cases", then click "OK". Your filter variable will remain.

So far, you have the non-donors selected. We need to add the donors to complete the sample. Simply use the compute function to add your dependent variable and this filter variable together. Name the new variable "Selection".

Now check your work by running a cross tabulation between "Selection" and "Donor" (Exhibit 9.5).

There should be an equal number of donors and random non-donors. As you can see in the output, there are 21,641 cases coded "1" and 21,641 cases coded "0" for donor in the selection field.

After all of your independent and dependent variables are recoded and your selection pool is set, you are ready to begin modeling.

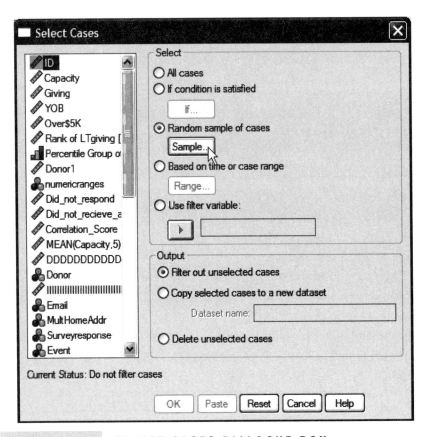

EXHIBIT 9.3   **SELECT CASES DIALOGUE BOX**

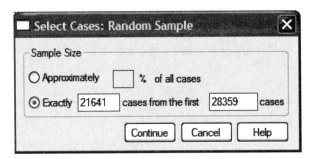

EXHIBIT 9.4   **SELECT CASES: RANDOM SAMPLE DIALOGUE BOX**

Count

		Selection		Total
		.00	1.00	
Donor	.00	6718	21641	28359
	1.00	0	21641	21641
Total		6718	43282	50000

EXHIBIT 9.5   **CROSS TABULATION OF DEPENDENT VARIABLE AND SELECTION VARIABLE**

MODELING

Select Analyze > Regression > Binary Logistic to open the dialogue box. Move "Donor" into the "Dependent" variable space. Move all of your independent variables into the "Covariates" space and move "Selection" into the "Selection Variable" space (Exhibit 9.6).

Next, click the "Rule" button next to the "Selection" variable space, type "1", and click to continue (Exhibit 9.7).

For now, leave the method on "Enter" and press "OK". SPSS will run for a while, depending on your file size. For this small a sample, it will only be a few seconds. Then SPSS will produce an output describing what it did. All of the terms and sections of the output are specifically defined in the help file on SPSS and in many statistics textbooks. I will point out elements worth the most attention.

By default, only some of the elements of the output will view. Additional information, such as "notes", will be available in the index on the left side. Double-click on "notes". The notes box simply describes what happened. It gives information such as the date, the location of the data file, the count of rows, the syntax for the operation, and the processing time.

Next on your output is the *Case Processing Summary* (Exhibit 9.8). This describes which cases were used in the analysis. As you can see, it used the 43,282 records we specified in our selection variable.

The next item on our output is the *Dependent Variable Encoding*. This simply says it dropped the decimals for our analysis (Exhibit 9.9).

After this, we have a very large section labeled, "Block 0: Beginning Block." If you recall the hat analogy from Chapter 3, you will remember

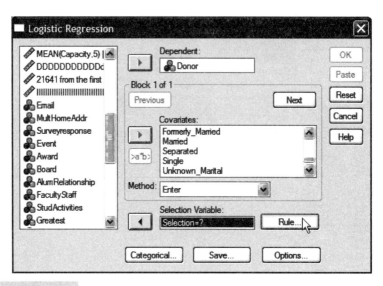

EXHIBIT 9.6   **LOGISTIC REGRESSION DIALOGUE BOX**

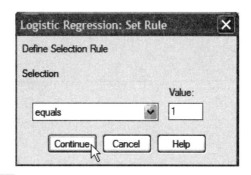

EXHIBIT 9.7   **SET RULE FOR SELECTION VARIABLE**

Case Processing Summary

Unweighted Cases [a]		N	Percent
Selected Cases	Included in Analysis	43282	86.6
	Missing Cases	0	.0
	Total	43282	86.6
Unselected Cases		6718	13.4
Total		50000	100.0

a. If weight is in effect, see classification table for the total number of cases.

EXHIBIT 9.8   **LOGISTIC REGRESSION OUTPUT: CASE PROCESSING SUMMARY**

Dependent Variable Encoding

Original Value	Internal Value
.00	0
1.00	1

EXHIBIT 9.9   **LOGISTIC REGRESSION OUTPUT: DEPENDENT VARIABLE ENCODING**

that the first step is pulling the major donor slips out of the hat and observing the other characteristics as you do it. Essentially, this is what the computer is doing in "Block 0". Most analysts scroll right past this block to evaluate their models. We will do the same.

Scroll to "Block 1: Method = Enter". This describes the process of trying to draw major donors out of the hat at a better rate than random by using a combination of the independent variables. The measure of beating random is the "Chi-square". The first element in "Block 1" is the "Omnibus Tests of Model Coefficients", which show us the Chi-square, the degrees of freedom, and the significance of the model. Pay attention to the Chi-square of each model you create by type. The higher the Chi-square while also being appropriately significant (below .05), the better (Exhibit 9.10).

The next output table is the *Model Summary*. This table gives you metrics that measure how much the model impacts the variance in your data. It is good to learn the R Square statistics if you plan on regular statistics work. For binary logistic regression, it is not the most effective measure, except to compare models. Most analysts actually skip right past this to the next section (Exhibit 9.11).

Omnibus Tests of Model Coefficients

		Chi-square	df	Sig.
Step 1	Step	12241.045	21	.000
	Block	12241.045	21	.000
	Model	12241.045	21	.000

EXHIBIT 9.10   **LOGISTIC REGRESSION OUTPUT: OMNIBUS TEST OF MODEL COEFFICIENTS**

Model Summary

Step	-2 Log likelihood	Cox & Snell R Square	Nagelkerke R Square
1	47760.548[a]	.246	.328

a. Estimation terminated at iteration number 6 because parameter estimates changed by less than .001.

EXHIBIT 9.11   **LOGISTIC REGRESSION OUTPUT: MODEL SUMMARY**

One of the most important tables to view in your output, and the first stopping point for most analysts, is the *Classification Table*. The formula of the model builds a probability score represented as a percentage. If we have a split file of donors and non-donors, cases with about 50% and higher probabilities might be considered "predicted to be donors." Cases with less than 50% probabilities might be considered "predicted to not be donors." Classification tables are cross tabs between actual donors and what the model predicted using the independent characteristics (Exhibit 9.12).

In this classification table, the predicted donor shows the 20,580 cases the model predicted would be donors. It was correct about 14,885 or 68.8% of current, observed donors. The other 5,695 are the false positives, also known as Type I errors. Of the cases it predicted would not be donors, it was correct about 15,946 or 73.7% of them. The other 6,756 are the false negatives, also known as Type II errors. The overall percentage is the average of the predicted correct percentages. The Unselected

Classification Table[c]

			Predicted					
			Selected Cases[a]			Unselected Cases[b]		
			Donor		Percentage Correct	Donor		Percentage Correct
Observed			.00	1.00		.00	1.00	
Step 1	Donor	.00	15946	5695	73.7	4923	1795	73.3
		1.00	6756	14885	68.8	0	0	.
	Overall Percentage				71.2			73.3

a. Selected cases Selection EQ 1

b. Unselected cases Selection NE 1

c. The cut value is .500

EXHIBIT 9.12   **LOGISTIC REGRESSION OUTPUT: CLASSIFICATION TABLE**

Variables in the Equation

		B	S.E.	Wald	df	Sig.	Exp(B)
Step 1[a]	Email	.594	.027	483.855	1	.000	1.811
	MultHomeAddr	.455	.199	5.214	1	.022	1.576
	Surveyresponse	-1.170	.025	2144.110	1	.000	.310
	Event	.470	.036	168.789	1	.000	1.601
	Award	.489	.437	1.251	1	.263	1.630
	Board	1.636	.419	15.237	1	.000	5.133
	AlumRelationship	.405	.039	106.214	1	.000	1.499
	FacultyStaff	-1.004	.074	185.725	1	.000	.367
	StudActivities	.078	.041	3.720	1	.054	1.081
	Greatest	.806	.040	414.257	1	.000	2.239
	GenX	-.662	.039	284.527	1	.000	.516
	Boomer	.260	.035	55.459	1	.000	1.297
	Millennial	-2.283	.104	486.017	1	.000	.102
	Award_Board	-.682	.441	2.391	1	.122	.506
	Divorced	.410	.247	2.759	1	.097	1.507
	Domestic_Partner	1.294	.255	25.719	1	.000	3.648
	Formerly_Married	.450	.874	.265	1	.607	1.568
	Married	.417	.135	9.574	1	.002	1.518
	Separated	.774	.680	1.295	1	.255	2.168
	Single	-.082	.140	.345	1	.557	.921
	Unknown_Marital	-.940	.135	48.318	1	.000	.391
	Constant	.658	.137	23.224	1	.000	1.932

a. Variable(s) entered on step 1: Email, MultHomeAddr, Surveyresponse, Event, Award, Board, AlumRelationship, FacultyStaff, StudActivities, Greatest, GenX, Boomer, Millennial, Award_Board, Divorced, Domestic_Partner, Formerly_Married, Married, Separated, Single, Unknown_Marital.

EXHIBIT 9.13   **LOGISTIC REGRESSION OUTPUT: VARIABLES IN THE EQUATION**

Cases section records where the records outside of our sample fell when you applied the formula to them.

It is a goal of logistic regression to maximize the percentage correct while having all variables in appropriate levels of significance. To see each of the variables used in the model, refer to the next table in the output, called *Variables in the Equation* (Exhibit 9.13).

This table lists the variables used in the model. The first column, labeled *B*, is the coefficient used for each variable. This shows the forward or inverse direction each variable contributed to the model. The final column, *Exp(B)*, is the exponent of the coefficient. Both of these fields show an amount of impact each variable has on a score. The second column, *S.E.*, is the standard of error, which is used to create the *Wald* Chi-square statistic in the next column. The significance of the Wald Chi-square statistic is the next column, labeled *Sig*. The Sig. column and the classification table will be where you look the most often. Your goal is to make sure each significance is below 0.05 to accept the variable in your model.

In our model, you can see there are several of the variables outside of the acceptable level of significance. These variables are Award, Student Activities, Award_Board, Divorced, Formerly Married, Separated, and Single. The best thing to do now is to rerun the model excluding these variables. Next, review the output for any variable still outside the acceptable level of significance. You may reintroduce some that you have excluded to see if they become significant when included with a different group of variables. When you have all of your variables below 0.05, and your classification table has the highest prediction percentages, you are nearly done with the model.

If you pursue this manual effort of removing variables with each run, you will find it takes a long time. SPSS makes this easier for you by running several of the steps for you. It offers three forward stepwise and three backward stepwise options. Forward is starting small and adding variables until you get the best model. Backward is starting with all of the variables and peeling away those that don't work for the model. What I have described manually is a backward stepwise method, making choices based on the significance of the Wald Chi-square.

To have SPSS run a stepwise method, simply run the regression formula again, but this time choose a method. I will demonstrate a Backward: Wald (Exhibit 9.14).

After selecting the method, click on the "Options" button and select "Display: At last step". This way, if SPSS takes many steps, you will not be scrolling through an overwhelming output full of steps. Click to continue and click "OK" (Exhibit 9.15).

Now review your output. It might still have a handful of variables outside of significance. If so, you might need to still conduct a few manual steps to remove them. Exhibit 9.16 is a list of variables from our final step. These will work for our model.

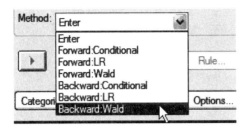

EXHIBIT 9.14 **LOGISTIC REGRESSION METHOD SELECTION OPTIONS**

In reviewing the classification table, we have a good percentage correct for this sample file (Exhibit 9.17).

Now, we are ready to score our model with this formula. To create a column with the probabilities from our model, simply run the regression formula again. This time, click the "Save" button and check the "Predicted Values: Probabilities" checkbox. Click to continue and click "OK" (Exhibit 9.18).

EXHIBIT 9.15 **LOGISTIC REGRESSION OPTIONS DIALOGUE BOX**

Variables in the Equation

		B	S.E.	Wald	df	Sig.	Exp(B)
Step 6[a]	Email	.596	.027	489.067	1	.000	1.816
	MultHomeAddr	.460	.199	5.345	1	.021	1.583
	Surveyresponse	-1.165	.025	2152.656	1	.000	.312
	Event	.477	.036	174.901	1	.000	1.612
	Board	1.205	.145	68.917	1	.000	3.338
	AlumRelationship	.413	.039	111.913	1	.000	1.511
	FacultyStaff	-1.008	.074	187.377	1	.000	.365
	Greatest	.811	.040	420.248	1	.000	2.249
	GenX	-.661	.039	285.734	1	.000	.517
	Boomer	.260	.035	55.713	1	.000	1.297
	Millennial	-2.280	.103	485.598	1	.000	.102
	Award_Board	-.186	.059	10.143	1	.001	.830
	Divorced	.479	.211	5.168	1	.023	1.614
	Domestic_Partner	1.361	.220	38.228	1	.000	3.899
	Married	.487	.041	141.637	1	.000	1.627
	Unknown_Marital	-.871	.040	477.451	1	.000	.419
	Constant	.589	.048	148.000	1	.000	1.803

a. Variable(s) entered on step 1: Email, MultHomeAddr, Surveyresponse, Event, Award, Board, AlumRelationship, FacultyStaff, Greatest, GenX, Boomer, Millennial, Award_Board, Divorced, Domestic_Partner, Formerly_ Married, Married, Separated, Single, Unknown_Marital.

EXHIBIT 9.16 **LOGISTIC REGRESSION OUTPUT: FINAL STEP OF VARIABLES IN THE EQUATION**

Classification Table[c]

			Predicted					
			Selected Cases[a]			Unselected Cases[b]		
			Donor		Percentage	Donor		Percentage
	Observed		.00	1.00	Correct	.00	1.00	Correct
Step 1	Donor	.00	16008	5633	74.0	4942	1776	73.6
		1.00	6790	14851	68.6	0	0	
	Overall Percentage				71.3			73.6
Step 6	Donor	.00	16010	5631	74.0	4942	1776	73.6
		1.00	6791	14850	68.6	0	0	
	Overall Percentage				71.3			73.6

a. Selected cases Selection EQ 1

b. Unselected cases Selection NE 1

c. The cut value is .500

EXHIBIT 9.17 **LOGISTIC REGRESSION OUTPUT: CLASSIFICATION TABLE WITH FIRST AND FINAL STEP**

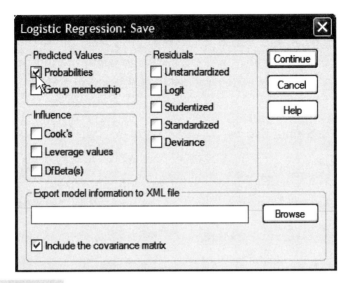

EXHIBIT 9.18   LOGISTIC REGRESSION SAVE DIALOGUE BOX

SPSS will append a column of probabilities to the end of your data-sheet. These values are very specific. They are likely too specific to evaluate and implement without recoding them. The next steps will convert these raw probabilities into more usable scores.

Creating a 0–1000 Score

To convert the probability from a decimal into a "0–1000" score, simply open Transform > Compute Variable and move the predicted probability score into the "Numeric Expression" space. Type or click "★" and type "1000" so the numeric expression reads, "PRE_1★1000". Name your variable "Score". Then click "OK". This will move the decimal. To remove the values to the right of the decimal, the quickest way is to click into the "Variable View" at the bottom of your window, change the variable type to a string, and click "OK". Finally, click on the variable type again and change it back to a numeric variable. The process of changing to a string will remove these values to the left of the decimal.

Creating an Ordinal Score

Another way of simplifying the score is to group it into quintiles or deciles. To do this, select Transform > Rank Cases. Move your predicted probability into the "Variable(s)" space and click the "Rank Types" button. Uncheck the "Rank" checkbox and check the "Ntiles" checkbox. Type in your number of groups, click to continue, and click "OK". SPSS will create a new ordinal variable at the end of your datasheet.

Creating Fractional Scores

When students take standardized tests, the scores do not reflect percentages correct but relative position. A 90% on a standardized test means that the student did better than 90% of the population. For some models, including major giving models, it is advisable to calculate a fractional percentage. To do this in SPSS, select Transform > Rank Cases. Move your predicted probability into the "Variable(s)" space and click the "Rank Types" button. Uncheck the "Rank" checkbox and check the "Fractional rank as percent" checkbox. Click to continue and click "OK". You may wish to convert this fractional rank to a "0–1000" score following the process outlined previously.

When making a model with a very small dependent variables, such as major giving, planned giving, or volunteer likelihood, I will recode the fractional rank into top-heavy ordinal rankings such as follows:

- 1 = Lower 49.9%
- 2 = 50–74.9%
- 2 = 75–89.9%
- 3 = 90–94.9%
- 4 = 95–97.49%
- 5 = 97.5–98.9%
- 6 = 99–99.49%
- 7 = 99.5–99.749%
- 8 = 99.75–99.89%
- 9 = Top 0.1%

In prospecting, your focus will be on the very top percentages. This score enables great division within the top 5% of constituents by likelihood to give major gifts. For most annual giving models, this type of ranking is unnecessary.

MODEL EVALUATION

A big part of the modeling process is evaluating the output measurements to rerun the model. After you are finished with the model, you should return to your original context to evaluate your scores. In Chapter 8, I presented a correlation ranking model by combining the top correlated factors into a point score. When we reviewed the cross tabulation, the presence of donors increased as our score increased. Exhibit 9.19 is that cross tabulation.

A challenge with this approach was the relatively few individuals with high scores. Also, we had little flexibility making cut values at difference percentages. Compare that to a cross tabulation of our regression model ranked into five groups and using the same data file and the same donor variable (Exhibit 9.20).

				Donor		
				.00	1.00	Total
Correlation_Score	.00	Count		389	120	509
		% within Correlation_Score		76.4%	23.6%	100.0%
	1.00	Count		10769	3673	14442
		% within Correlation_Score		74.6%	25.4%	100.0%
	2.00	Count		13641	12121	25762
		% within Correlation_Score		53.0%	47.0%	100.0%
	3.00	Count		3270	4212	7482
		% within Correlation_Score		43.7%	56.3%	100.0%
	4.00	Count		286	1319	1605
		% within Correlation_Score		17.8%	82.2%	100.0%
	5.00	Count		4	196	200
		% within Correlation_Score		2.0%	98.0%	100.0%
Total		Count		28359	21641	50000
		% within Correlation_Score		56.7%	43.3%	100.0%

EXHIBIT 9.19   CROSS TABULATION OF CORRELATION RANKING SCORE AND DONOR

Percentile Group of PRE_1 * Donor Cross Tabulation

			Donor		
			.00	1.00	Total
Percentile Group of PRE_1	1	Count	7801	1074	8875
		% within Percentile Group of PRE_1	87.9%	12.1%	100.0%
	2	Count	8600	2493	11093
		% within Percentile Group of PRE_1	77.5%	22.5%	100.0%
	3	Count	5791	4275	10066
		% within Percentile Group of PRE_1	57.5%	42.5%	100.0%
	4	Count	4232	5879	10111
		% within Percentile Group of PRE_1	41.9%	58.1%	100.0%
	5	Count	1935	7920	9855
		% within Percentile Group of PRE_1	19.6%	80.4%	100.0%
Total		Count	28359	21641	50000
		% within Percentile Group of PRE_1	56.7%	43.3%	100.0%

EXHIBIT 9.20   CROSS TABULATION OF REGRESSION ANALYSIS RANKING AND DONOR

You can see that the model has the same progression upwards by percentages of donors by group; however, the sizes of the groups are significantly different. These following charts illustrate this difference. Although both have similar percentages correct by score, only the regression formula accomplishes this while having a smooth distribution by the count of donors (Exhibits 9.21 and 9.22).

Because the regression formula provides precision to multiple decimals, it is easy to select an exact percentage of records for an appeal. Not only does the distribution of actual donors by score surpass the correlation ranking, but so do the correlation statistics. The correlation score had a Spearman correlation of .264. The Spearman correlation statistic for the regression formula was .485 (Exhibit 9.23).

For overall giving models, comparing to the actual existing behavior is the most important evaluation step. You might also send a random sample of never-donor appeals, and evaluate future response based on the model. The best evaluation is test implementation.

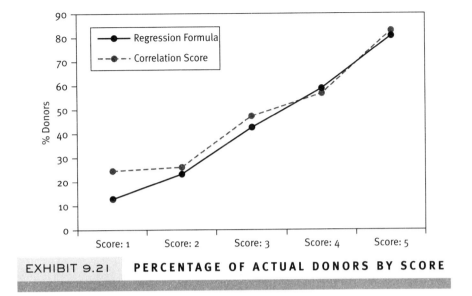

EXHIBIT 9.21   PERCENTAGE OF ACTUAL DONORS BY SCORE

For all models, refer back to the original business context. With major and planned giving models, you should compare the results to existing major donors, managed prospects, and qualified suspects. Also, have prospect identification specialists spot-check the top unmanaged scores. Their

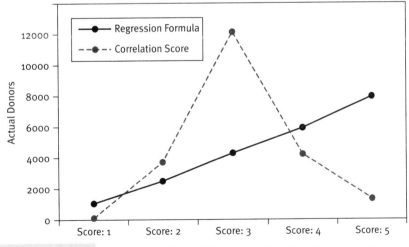

EXHIBIT 9.22   COUNT OF ACTUAL DONORS BY SCORE

Symmetric Measures

		Value	Asymp. Std. Error[a]	Approx. T[b]	Approx. Sig.
Interval by Interval	Pearson's R	.485	.004	123.980	.000[c]
Ordinal by Ordinal	Spearman Correlation	.485	.004	123.982	.000[c]
N of Valid Cases		50000			

a. Not assuming the null hypothesis.

b. Using the asymptotic standard error assuming the null hypothesis.

c. Based on normal approximation.

EXHIBIT 9.23   CORRELATION STATISTICS FOR CROSS TABULATION OF REGRESSION ANALYSIS RANKING AND DONOR

success in qualifying these prospects is the best test implementation for models of this variety.

FINAL THOUGHTS ON PREDICTIVE MODELING

I am a firm believer that the best way to learn is to do. Many different models are variations on a theme. By working your way through prepping a file and producing a score using this binary logistic regression example, you are 90% of the way toward building other model varieties. With ample doses of curiosity and resolve, you will become an analytics wizard.

As long as you always start with the Cross Industry Standard Process for Data Mining (CRISP-DM) and conduct your analysis in the context of your business purpose, you will hammer through and achieve the goal. I have consulted many fundraisers in statistics. I have also consulted many statisticians in fundraising. By far, it is easier for fundraisers to be successful when they are armed with the knowledge of context and implementation than it is for statisticians armed only with technology. When knowledge and technology come together, the potential is limitless.

Explore your software options. Meet with your data services, annual giving, and research teams. Plan your modeling strategy. It will not be an overnight process. Begin by building one model and seeing it all the way through implementation. Document your successes and failures. Then present the impact to your fundraising program leaders. I would be surprised if they are not impressed. I think you will be impressed, too.

Final Thoughts on Fundraising Analytics

I have a daughter who recently learned how to read. At home she learned to sing through her ABCs. In preschool, she learned how to recognize and write all of the letters. In kindergarten, she started to combine the letters and sound out the words. I remember her teachers and our family working with her as she learned these basics of language. It seemed like such a struggle for her until one day, she just seemed to get it.

Ever since, she has been hungry for reading. We cannot pass a sign without her stopping to sound out the words. After tackling one "easy reader," she moves right on to the next one. Her room has become a library. She was even looking over my shoulder as I typed many of the sections in this book.

You will see this zeal in a child when they first learn to ride a bike. They will stay out until dusk to enjoy their new freedom of motion. When they learn to read musical notes on the piano, they will play away without thought of sleeping babies or exhausted parents. There are some things you learn that open a whole new world you never realized was there.

For me, analytics was one of these eye-opening experiences. It might seem like just numbers on the surface. I am sure my daughter only saw the letters before the words came together. Eventually, these numbers will come together for you, and your world will change. You will tap into a tremendous potential in your database. You will be surprised what is in that world when it opens up.

I hope *Fundraising Analytics* brought you a bit closer to this possibility. Before long, you will be mining every bit of data you can find. You will dive into a world of discovery to understand the unique diversity of your donors. Curiosity will take over, and the ease you will have in answering those questions will be magical. It will seem as if your donors have another means of communicating with you. They will talk to you through your data.

Thank you for joining me on this journey. May your donors know you really hear them.

Glossary of Common Analytics Terminology

Affinity   Having positive feelings about an institution. Generally, giving affinity comes from earned loyalty.

Analytics   A suite of statistical tools and techniques used to:

- Analyze constituencies
- Build models to predict constituent behaviors
- Make organizational decisions by:
  - Evaluating program performance
  - Projecting future program performance

Benchmarking   Comparing data in relevant categories against an established standard of success at similar institutions to determine relative performance.

Campaign Pyramid   A very common campaign planning tool, the campaign pyramid is a spreadsheet or series of spreadsheets listing the gifts needed by level, the prospects needed to achieve the gifts, and the suspects needed to qualify the prospects.

Capacity   The ultimate amount of money a constituent could give in five years in an ideal scenario.

Capacity Yield   A comparison of giving to the rated capacity of the prospect. Typically, a capacity yield is produced using the previous five years' giving in relation to a five-year giving capacity score.

Channel   Vehicles of interaction whereby a donor might give a gift. Common channels include direct mail, phone, online, and in-person.

Cluster Analysis   Grouping individuals and corporations together in ways that might not be obvious to you using data mining. Common types include Two-Step and K-Means.

Correlation   A measurement of the relationship between two random variables that can be expressed numerically.

CRISP-DM   Cross-Industry Standard Process for Data Mining, characterized by six stages:

- *Business Understanding:* Defining the context of the analysis
- *Data Understanding:* Aligning data elements to the context

- *Data Preparation:* Gathering and priming the data for analysis
- *Modeling:* Conducting the analysis
- *Evaluation:* Determining if the analysis supports the goal of the business understanding
- *Deployment:* Implementing the analysis

Cross Tabulation   A comparison of the values of two fields to observe overlapping values.

Data Mining   Finding useful information by identifying patterns and trends within large databases. Often, this statistical pattern recognition is married with predictive analytics to produce predictive models.

Decision Logic/Decision Support   Metrics-based forecasting and simulation studies to determine database potential, capacity, or philanthropic potential of constituent segments and investment priorities.

Demographics   The characteristics of individuals within a population (such as age, gender, nationality, marital status, etc.) that may be analyzed for informational or predictive purposes.

Dependent Variable   The behavior or value to be measured, evaluated, or modeled in a data mining project.

Descriptive Analytics   Analyzing constituencies to understand core segments according to behaviors and demographics. Also, analyzing programs to understand performance and the key factors and metrics impacting this performance.

Forecasting   Using metrical analysis of known data to predict future results.

Frequency Distribution   A count and percentage of the cases coded with each of the distinct values within a field.

Giving Motivations/Philanthropic Motivations   Why donors give gifts. Primary motivations include:

- Loyalty
- Global impact
- Personal interest
- Duty
- Empathy

Hard Credit   Giving amounts actually given by a donor and credited for tax purposes.

Independent Variables   Characteristics existing separate from the dependent variable used in data mining projects to develop patterns and predict the dependent variable.

LYBUNT   Acronym, meaning gave Last Year But Unfortunately Not This year. This donor segment refers to the annual giving donors scheduled for renewal.

Mean   Average: Sum of the values in a series divided by the count of cases in the series.

Median   The value of the case where an equal number of values of the other cases in the series are both higher and lower.

Metrical Analysis   Evaluating multiple variables within a database to develop a data-informed understanding of a program or process.

Mode   The most recurring value in a series of values.

Nominal   Also called categorical or logistic, nominal variable values represent categories with no intrinsic ranking; for example, the department of the company in which an employee works. Examples of nominal variables include yes/no variables, channels, volunteers, gender, marital status, region, ZIP code, and religious affiliation.

Ordinal   The values of ordinal variables represent categories with some intrinsic ranking; for example, levels of service satisfaction from highly dissatisfied to highly satisfied. Examples of ordinal variables include attitude scores representing degree of satisfaction or confidence, preference ranking scores, "A, B, C" propensity rankings, and gift levels.

Predictive Analytics   Using internal and/or external data to predict behaviors and segment constituents according to probabilities.

Predictive Modeling   An outcome of predictive analytics, predictive models are formulas producing probability scores predicting future behaviors. Typically, these are built using statistical tools such as regression analysis, decision trees, and neural networks.

Profiling   Determining characteristics and motivations of particular groups within a larger set using data categories common to that group.

Propensity   Likelihood or willingness to give a gift to an institution.

Prospect Management   A systematized process of identifying constituents with the potential for major giving; engaging them with appropriate strategies; maintaining a confidence in your institution's worthiness; maintaining dedicated focus on case-stating; soliciting prospects for gifts; and stewarding them by acknowledging their gifts, recognizing their impact on the organization, and keeping them informed about the ongoing benefits of their contributions.

Prospecting   Fundraising business process for finding individuals in the base of support and feeding them into the major giving pipeline.

Regression Analysis   Regression analysis is a method of analysis where a behavior or value is observed or "predicted" by evaluating characteristics independent of the behavior. The outcome of such analysis is a probability of a case engaging in the behavior or a predicted amount for a value.

RFM Analysis   A measurement of customer or constituent value. In fundraising, it refers to how recently a donor gave, how frequently they give, and how much they gave.

Scale   A variable can be treated as a scale when its values are represented linearly, so that distance comparisons between values are appropriate. Examples of scale variables include total giving dollars, attachment scores, RFM scores, age in years, and capacity in dollars.

Segmentation   Statistically analyzing variables within a database to categorize individuals according to similar characteristics.

Simulation   Adjusting known data to understand the effect of variables on areas of program performance.

Soft Credit   Giving amounts credited to a donor for stewardship purposes, although the tax credit belongs to another entity, such as a spouse or a company.

SYBUNT Acronym, meaning gave Some Year But Unfortunately Not This year. This lapsed donor segment refers to the annual giving donors scheduled for reactivation.

Text Mining Text mining is a method of extracting value from free text data. Many large-scale survey researchers will search for common phrases and terms in free text response to measure against behaviors.

Trend General movement of data in any direction over time.

Type I Errors When comparing actual to predicted values in a regression formula classification table, Type I errors refer to the false positives.

Type II Errors When comparing actual to predicted values in a regression formula classification table, Type II errors refer to the false negatives.

Value Portfolio A grouping of things, people, interests, or ideas cherished by an individual. People's value portfolios might include their home, their community, an heirloom, their significant other, their children, all children, the poor, peace, education, religion, artistic expression, health, or any thing else of value to them.

AFP Code of Ethical Principles and Standards

ETHICAL PRINCIPLES • Adopted 1964; amended Sept. 2007

The Association of Fundraising Professionals (AFP) exists to foster the development and growth of fundraising professionals and the profession, to promote high ethical behavior in the fundraising profession and to preserve and enhance philanthropy and volunteerism. Members of AFP are motivated by an inner drive to improve the quality of life through the causes they serve. They serve the ideal of philanthropy, are committed to the preservation and enhancement of volunteerism; and hold stewardship of these concepts as the overriding direction of their professional life. They recognize their responsibility to ensure that needed resources are vigorously and ethically sought and that the intent of the donor is honestly fulfilled. To these ends, AFP members, both individual and business, embrace certain values that they strive to uphold in performing their responsibilities for generating philanthropic support. AFP business members strive to promote and protect the work and mission of their client organizations.

AFP members both individual and business aspire to:

- practice their profession with integrity, honesty, truthfulness and adherence to the absolute obligation to safeguard the public trust
- act according to the highest goals and visions of their organizations, professions, clients and consciences
- put philanthropic mission above personal gain;
- inspire others through their own sense of dedication and high purpose
- improve their professional knowledge and skills, so that their performance will better serve others
- demonstrate concern for the interests and well-being of individuals affected by their actions
- value the privacy, freedom of choice and interests of all those affected by their actions
- foster cultural diversity and pluralistic values and treat all people with dignity and respect
- affirm, through personal giving, a commitment to philanthropy and its role in society
- adhere to the spirit as well as the letter of all applicable laws and regulations
- advocate within their organizations adherence to all applicable laws and regulations
- avoid even the appearance of any criminal offense or professional misconduct
- bring credit to the fundraising profession by their public demeanor
- encourage colleagues to embrace and practice these ethical principles and standards
- be aware of the codes of ethics promulgated by other professional organizations that serve philanthropy

ETHICAL STANDARDS

Furthermore, while striving to act according to the above values, AFP members, both individual and business, agree to abide (and to ensure, to the best of their ability, that all members of their staff abide) by the AFP standards. Violation of the standards may subject the member to disciplinary sanctions, including expulsion, as provided in the AFP Ethics Enforcement Procedures.

MEMBER OBLIGATIONS

1. Members shall not engage in activities that harm the members' organizations, clients or profession.
2. Members shall not engage in activities that conflict with their fiduciary, ethical and legal obligations to their organizations, clients or profession.
3. Members shall effectively disclose all potential and actual conflicts of interest; such disclosure does not preclude or imply ethical impropriety.
4. Members shall not exploit any relationship with a donor, prospect, volunteer, client or employee for the benefit of the members or the members' organizations.
5. Members shall comply with all applicable local, state, provincial and federal civil and criminal laws.
6. Members recognize their individual boundaries of competence and are forthcoming and truthful about their professional experience and qualifications and will represent their achievements accurately and without exaggeration.
7. Members shall present and supply products and/or services honestly and without misrepresentation and will clearly identify the details of those products, such as availability of the products and/or services and other factors that may affect the suitability of the products and/or services for donors, clients or nonprofit organizations.
8. Members shall establish the nature and purpose of any contractual relationship at the outset and will be responsive and available to organizations and their employing organizations before, during and after any sale of materials and/or services. Members will comply with all fair and reasonable obligations created by the contract.
9. Members shall refrain from knowingly infringing the intellectual property rights of other parties at all times. Members shall address and rectify any inadvertent infringement that may occur.
10. Members shall protect the confidentiality of all privileged information relating to the provider/client relationships.
11. Members shall refrain from any activity designed to disparage competitors untruthfully.

SOLICITATION AND USE OF PHILANTHROPIC FUNDS

12. Members shall take care to ensure that all solicitation and communication materials are accurate and correctly reflect their organizations' mission and use of solicited funds.
13. Members shall take care to ensure that donors receive informed, accurate and ethical advice about the value and tax implications of contributions.
14. Members shall take care to ensure that contributions are used in accordance with donors' intentions.
15. Members shall take care to ensure proper stewardship of all revenue sources, including timely reports on the use and management of such funds.
16. Members shall obtain explicit consent by donors before altering the conditions of financial transactions.

PRESENTATION OF INFORMATION

17. Members shall not disclose privileged or confidential information to unauthorized parties.
18. Members shall adhere to the principle that all donor and prospect information created by, or on behalf of, an organization or a client is the property of that organization or client and shall not be transferred or utilized except on behalf of that organization or client.
19. Members shall give donors and clients the opportunity to have their names removed from lists that are sold to, rented to or exchanged with other organizations.
20. Members shall, when stating fundraising results, use accurate and consistent accounting methods that conform to the appropriate guidelines adopted by the American Institute of Certified Public Accountants (AICPA)* for the type of organization involved. (* In countries outside of the United States, comparable authority should be utilized.)

COMPENSATION AND CONTRACTS

21. Members shall not accept compensation or enter into a contract that is based on a percentage of contributions; nor shall members accept finder's fees or contingent fees. Business members must refrain from receiving compensation from third parties derived from products or services for a client without disclosing that third-party compensation to the client (for example, volume rebates from vendors to business members).
22. Members may accept performance-based compensation, such as bonuses, provided such bonuses are in accord with prevailing practices within the members' own organizations and are not based on a percentage of contributions.
23. Members shall neither offer nor accept payments or special considerations for the purpose of influencing the selection of products or services.
24. Members shall not pay finder's fees, commissions or percentage compensation based on contributions, and shall take care to discourage their organizations from making such payments.
25. Any member receiving funds on behalf of a donor or client must meet the legal requirements for the disbursement of those funds. Any interest or income earned on the funds should be fully disclosed.

A Donor Bill of Rights

PHILANTHROPY is based on voluntary action for the common good. It is a tradition of giving and sharing that is primary to the quality of life. To assure that philanthropy merits the respect and trust of the general public, and that donors and prospective donors can have full confidence in the not-for-profit organizations and causes they are asked to support, we declare that all donors have these rights:

I.

To be informed of the organization's mission, of the way the organization intends to use donated resources, and of its capacity to use donations effectively for their intended purposes.

II.

To be informed of the identity of those serving on the organization's governing board, and to expect the board to exercise prudent judgement in its stewardship responsibilities.

III.

To have access to the organization's most recent financial statements.

IV.

To be assured their gifts will be used for the purposes for which they were given.

V.

To receive appropriate acknowledgement and recognition.

VI.

To be assured that information about their donations is handled with respect and with confidentiality to the extent provided by law.

VII.

To expect that all relationships with individuals representing organizations of interest to the donor will be professional in nature.

VIII.

To be informed whether those seeking donations are volunteers, employees of the organization or hired solicitors.

IX.

To have the opportunity for their names to be deleted from mailing lists that an organization may intend to share.

X.

To feel free to ask questions when making a donation and to receive prompt, truthful and forthright answers.

DEVELOPED BY
Association for Healthcare Philanthropy (AHP)
Association of Fundraising Professionals (AFP)
Council for Advancement and Support of Education (CASE)
Giving Institute: Leading Consultants to Non-Profits

ENDORSED BY
(in formation)
Independent Sector
National Catholic Development Conference (NCDC)
National Committee on Planned Giving (NCPG)
Council for Resource Development (CRD)
United Way of America

Index